The Mountaintop

Katori Hall is from Memphis, Tennessee. Her play *The Mountaintop* was first produced to great acclaim at Theatre503, London, in June 2009, and received a transfer to the Trafalgar Studios, London, the following month. It won the Olivier Award for Best New Play in 2010, and opened in Broadway's Bernard B. Jacobs Theatre, New York City, in October 2011. Other plays include *Hurt Village*, *Hoodoo Love*, *Remembrance*, *S aturday Night/Sunday Morning*, *WHADDABLOODCLOT!!!*, *The Hope Well* and *Pussy Valley*. Her numerous awards include the 2007 Fellowship of Southern Writers Bryan Family Award in Drama, a 2006 New York Foundation of the Arts Fellowship in Playwriting and Screenwriting, a residency at the Royal Court Theatre in 2006, and the 2005 Lorraine Hansberry Playwriting award.

Harvey Young is Dean of the College of Fine Arts and Professor of English and Theatre at Boston University, USA. A cultural historian, he is the author/editor of ten books, including *Theatre & Race* and *Embodying Black Experience*.

T0244928

The Mountaintop

KATORI HALL

With commentary and notes by
HARVEY YOUNG

Series Editors:
Jenny Stevens, Matthew Nichols, Sara Freeman
and Chris Megson

methuen | drama

LONDON • NEW YORK • OXFORD • NEW DELHI • SYDNEY

METHUEN DRAMA
Bloomsbury Publishing Plc
50 Bedford Square, London, WC1B 3DP, UK
1385 Broadway, New York, NY 10018, USA
29 Earlsfort Terrace, Dublin 2, Ireland

BLOOMSBURY, METHUEN DRAMA and the Methuen Drama logo are trademarks of
Bloomsbury Publishing Plc

First published in Great Britain in 2011 by Methuen Drama

This edition is published by Bloomsbury Methuen Drama 2015

A catalogue record for this book is available from the British Library.

Library of Congress Cataloging-in-Publication Data
Names: Hall, Katori, author. | Young, Harvey, 1975- writer of added commentary.
Title: The mountaintop / Katori Hall; with commentary and notes by Harvey Young.
Description: London; New York: Methuen Drama, 2024. | Series: Student editions
Identifiers: LCCN 2023030923 (print) | LCCN 2023030924 (ebook) |
ISBN 9781350187955 (paperback) | ISBN 9781350187962 (pdf) | ISBN 9781350187979 (epub)
Subjects: LCSH: King, Martin Luther, Jr., 1929-1968–Drama. |
Memphis (Tenn.)–Drama. | LCGFT: Biographical drama.
Classification: LCC PS3608.A54727 M68 2024 (print) | LCC PS3608.A54727 (ebook) |
DDC 812/.6–dc23/eng/20230719
LC record available at https://lccn.loc.gov/2023030923
LC ebook record available at https://lccn.loc.gov/2023030924

ISBN: PB: 978-1-3501-8795-5
ePDF: 978-1-3501-8796-2
eBook: 978-1-3501-8797-9

Series: Student Editions

Typeset by Deanta Global Publishing Services, Chennai, India
Printed and bound in Great Britain

To find out more about our authors and books visit www.bloomsbury.com
and sign up for our newsletters.

Contents

Introduction

It is nearly impossible to think about the mid-twentieth-century Civil Rights Movement in the United States without imagining the face or hearing the voice of Reverend Dr. Martin Luther King, Jr. King, the trailblazing African American preacher and social activist with a pencil moustache and a booming baritone, stood at the centre of many of the most iconic moments in the civil rights struggle. In the collective remembering of the Movement, he is omnipresent. There he stands on the steps of the Lincoln Memorial in Washington, DC, in 1963, sharing his dream of children being judged by the 'content of their character' and 'not by . . . the color of their skin'.[1] There he marches through city streets in an effort to spotlight and dismantle segregationist systems. Always working in concert with others, he nevertheless, stands apart. The effectiveness of his prose and his philosophy of peaceful, non-violent protest in the face of hostility made him a uniquely inspiring leader.

It is a testament to the vibrant life and extraordinary impact of Martin Luther King, Jr., that his actions and activism continue to resonate more than a half-century after his death. We remember him for his deeds and his good work in support of marginalized and underprivileged communities. Since his murder by an assassin's bullet on 4 April 1968, the legacy of Martin Luther King, Jr. has been preserved. In 1983, his birthday became an official US holiday and remains one of only three federal holidays in honour of an individual (alongside President George Washington and explorer Christopher Columbus). Numerous memorials have been erected across the United States to record and share King's legacy. More than one hundred US public schools bear his name.[2]

Katori Hall's *The Mountaintop* takes us back to the evening of 3 April 1968, the day before Martin Luther King, Jr. was murdered. Setting the play in King's room in the Lorraine Motel, Hall invites us to spend time with the civil rights leader on the eve of his assassination. The play itself is a work of fiction. Although there are numerous accounts of King's activities on 3 April 1968, none suggest that he spent the evening in conversation with a member of the Lorraine Motel staff. However, Hall's brilliant narrative framing – imagining the civil rights icon and a housekeeper in dialogue – gives us access to a moment in his life. It reveals King the man not the myth. He is all too human, replete with fears and desires.

Civil Rights Movement

The movement for civil rights within the United States, specifically the campaign for African Americans to have basic citizenship rights – individual liberty, property ownership and voting rights – is as old as the country itself. Although the framers of the Declaration of Independence, which outlined colonial America's aspirations to stand apart from Great Britain, asserted the importance of individual freedoms, they (all of whom were white men) chose not to recognize the rights and individual liberties of people who did not look like them. Following the successful conclusion of the American Revolution in 1783, these white men wrote and, through fledgling state legislatures, ratified a constitution that provided a governing framework for the nascent United States of America. The new document did not recognize the citizenship rights of women. It sanctioned slavery and identified African American captives, for the purpose of the census or population counts, as 'three-fifths' of a person. The effort to amend the constitution and correct the oversights as well as outright prejudices of the 'founding fathers' would begin almost immediately. Nevertheless, it would still take another century to end slavery and for Black men to gain citizenship rights; and a further half-century, until 1919, for women to be granted the right to vote.

The herculean effort to shift the country from founding principles of exclusion and marginalization to one of inclusion and acceptance spanned centuries. It also required the efforts of countless individuals. Some of these trailblazers, like Martin Luther King, Jr., have been immortalized, but the majority of the individuals who championed and made progress possible remain unknown. For example, in 1929, when King was born in Atlanta, Georgia, the city already boasted a history of collective activism towards increased civil rights and liberties. Historian Clarissa Myrick-Harris writes, 'In July 1881 a group of 20 black washerwomen met in a church in Summerhill and established a labor organization called the Washing Society.'[3] She adds, 'Before the month was over, 3,000 women, including some white washerwomen, went on strike for better wages and more autonomy in their work.' The work of protest and activism was organized by community-based groups, especially churches.

There are innumerable moments that comprise the Civil Rights Movement in the United States. Among the activities most cited by historians, there was the founding of the Niagara Movement in 1905, which would eventually become the NAACP (National Association for the Advancement of Colored People) and would play a central role in organizing campaigns for equal rights across the country as well as leading the courtroom offensive to dismantle discriminatory policies and segregationist laws. There was the activism of Ida B. Wells among others against 'legal lynching': the unprosecuted murders of thousands of Black men and women throughout the late nineteenth century and early twentieth centuries. In addition, there were public demonstrations – sit-ins, boycotts and marches – designed to challenge the segregationist status quo. Rosa Parks, supported by the NAACP, deliberately sat and refused to relinquish her seat on a segregated bus and, in so doing, catalysed a thirteen-month-long bus boycott in Montgomery, Alabama.

The Civil Rights Movement is often considered to begin in 1955 with the decision of Mamie Till Mobley to display the bloated, disfigured body of her murdered thirteen-year-old son Emmett Till. Till was kidnapped in Mississippi and killed for whistling at a white woman. Supported by the emergent NAACP, Mobley chose to have an open-coffin funeral and invited the citizens of Chicago (her hometown) to look upon the body of her son. Newspapers reported on the courageous decision to show the body and reveal the horrors of mid-twentieth-century racism. *Jet*, a magazine, printed a photograph of the boy's face and launched a movement for social change throughout the country. Rosa Parks remembered Till when she remained sitting on that bus in Montgomery, Alabama. Her arrest for refusing to surrender her seat to a white passenger and the resulting yearlong boycott led to the desegregation of public transportation in the city. The end of the movement is most often associated with the assassination of Martin Luther King, Jr., which left the campaign for civil rights without a recognizable leader. It became rudderless.

Less than two decades long (but enabled by more than a century of activism, advocacy and campaigns), the American Civil Rights Movement brought about significant and lasting change within society. During this period, the violence that had targeted Black children, women and men since the seventeenth century was no longer deemed societally acceptable. Segregation and outright discrimination on the basis of race – in areas ranging from housing to education to the workplace – became unlawful and, indeed, unconstitutional. These changes occurred relatively swiftly within American society. However, it is important to remember that they also occurred not too long ago. The recent nature of the Civil Rights Movement helps to explain contemporary challenges and lingering hostilities related to ongoing integrationist efforts and campaigns for inclusion. There are folks who still remember with fondness the unevenly available and distributed privileges within society and covet a return to older (and, yes, racist) systems of social organization. As a result, vigilance is needed to protect and preserve the gains that were accomplished during the lifetime of Martin Luther King, Jr.

Martin, not Michael

As many people know, Martin Luther King, Jr., was named after his father Martin Luther King, Sr., a Baptist preacher who lived and preached in Atlanta, Georgia. Few people know that 'Martin' was neither of their birth names. Born on 15 January 1929 to Michael King and Alberta Christine Williams King, the young child who would later be known as Martin Luther King, Jr., spent the first five years of his life as Michael King, Jr. In 1934, during a visit to Germany and a witnessing of the escalating racist rhetoric of the rising fascist (Nazi) regime, King's father had an epiphany. Inspired by the legacy of Protestant reformer Martin Luther, King returned to Atlanta and shortly thereafter determined to change not only his own name but also his son's. Young Michael became Martin. However, 'close friends and relatives would continue to refer to [both] as Mike and M.L.'[4]

Decades later, in 1957 at the age of twenty-eight, the civil rights leader would legally change his name.

Martin Luther King, Jr., was raised within the Black church and, as a child, witnessed campaigns to address social inequalities. He attended Ebenezer Baptist Church, where both his father and grandfather presided as pastors. His father 'led marches and rallies to protest discriminatory social policies in Atlanta, including the desegregation of the Atlanta Police Department and the Atlanta Board of Education.'[5] King was a dedicated student and his studies at Morehouse College, Crozier Theological Seminary and Boston University (where he earned his doctorate) provided him with the complex blend of theology and philosophy that would inform his perspective on the world. For example, it was at Boston University in conversation with Dean Howard Thurman that he was encouraged to study the teaching of Eastern philosophy as a continued exploration of the power of non-violent demonstration. As a student in Boston, he met his future wife Coretta Scott, a music student at New England Conservatory.

Martin Luther King, Jr.'s rise within the Civil Rights Movement was swift. In 1955, the same year that he graduated from Boston University, he moved to Montgomery, Alabama. He lived in the city during the bus boycott and, by year's end, became the spokesperson for the Montgomery Improvement Association. Two years later, he would co-found the Southern Christian Leadership Conference, and by 1959, he had relocated to Atlanta, Georgia, where he would serve as a co-pastor at Ebenezer Baptist Church. In the first half of the 1960s, Martin Luther King, Jr., emerged as the most prominent and recognizable of his generation of civil rights leaders. He crisscrossed the country participating in marches and protests. Between 1960 and 1964, he regularly put his body on the line in support of civil rights and, as a result, was repeatedly arrested: in 1960 at a sit-in in Atlanta; in 1962 in Albany, Georgia; and in 1963 in Birmingham, Alabama. King's letter, written while incarcerated for eleven days in Birmingham, is now considered to be one of the most significant writings of the American civil rights era. In it, he not only diagnoses the bleak state – 'the hard, brutal, and unbelievable facts' – of racial discrimination in the American South but also articulates the moral and ethical imperative to address these wrongs.[6] King's activism, in concert with the strikers and others who took to the streets to boycott businesses and community restrictions, enabled desegregation to occur in Birmingham. In 1964, Martin Luther King, Jr., was widely honoured for his successes in challenging and leading the charge to dismantle segregationist systems. Among many accolades, he was awarded the Nobel Peace Prize, becoming the youngest person (aged thirty-five) to win the prize.

It is important to remember that the bulk of Martin Luther King, Jr.'s activism occurred *after* the US Supreme Court ruled against segregationist policies in 1955. Judicial decisions and rulings did not end racism or racist hostilities. There was considerable resistance to integrating schools, restaurants and governmental facilities. Restrictive covenants which prevented people with brown skin from residing in parts of a city continued. King, alongside innumerable others, sought to dismantle a system of disprivilege that disenfranchised African Americans. Although his leadership led to a series of successes such as the passage of federal laws to protect civil rights (Civil Rights Act in 1964) and to create safeguards on voter rights (Voting Rights Act in 1965), the implementation of those new laws required enforcement, monitoring and continued vigilance.

Having achieved success against segregationist systems across the country, Martin Luther King, Jr., began, by the mid-1960s, to address the problem of poverty within the United States. The campaign had its obvious roots in the country's long history of racial prejudice and discrimination. The institution of American chattel slavery, segregationist employment practices that limited African Americans to the lowest paying jobs and restrictions on housing as well as banking access resulted in considerable poverty within Black communities. King called for the creation of more jobs – a guaranteed income – for all citizens and launched a campaign for a dramatic redistribution of wealth. Referring to boycotts, sit-ins and strikes, he observed, 'It took a Birmingham before the government moved to open doors of public accommodations to all human beings. What we now needed was a new kind of Selma or Birmingham to dramatize the economic plight of the Negro, and compel the government to act'.[7] Plans were made for another gathering in Washington, DC, perhaps larger than the one that occurred in 1963. King imagined a more inclusive movement with 'representatives of the millions of non-Negro poor-Indians, Mexican Americans, Puerto Ricans, Appalachians, and others'.[8] He 'welcomed assistance from all Americans of goodwill'.[9]

When King arrived in Memphis, in 1968, in support of the ongoing strike of the city's trash collectors, his presence existed as both a continuation of the push for civil rights and the expanding anti-poverty efforts, the Poor People's Campaign, to ensure that all workers would have the benefit of a safe workplace and the dignity of a living wage. There were considerable pressures on King on this visit. A few weeks earlier, he had been in the city (also in support of the sanitation workers) and an episode of violence ended with a Black teenager killed by a police officer. Although the civil rights leader was quickly escorted away and protected from the violence, the chaos and death within a campaign designed to be peaceful and non-violent concerned him. Furthermore, there was a notable increase in death threats against him. Somehow, his efforts to redistribute wealth were deemed more threatening to people than his challenge to discriminatory systems. As King stood before those assembled at Mason Temple on the eve of his assassination, he likely thought about the disruptive presence of violence as well as the ongoing threats to his own life. Previously, in 1958, King had been stabbed in Harlem, New York. He had been struck in the head by a brick thrown at him during a march in Chicago, Illinois, in 1966. At Mason Temple, he shared a premonition: 'I've seen the promised land. I may not get there with you. But I want you to know tonight that we, as a people, will get to the promised land'.[10]

Lorraine Motel

The Lorraine Motel was Martin Luther King, Jr.'s preferred place to stay during his visits to Memphis, Tennessee. The aesthetics of the lodging establishment aligned with King's no fuss persona: the Lorraine Motel was far from a fancy establishment. However, it had the essentials for a weary traveller: bed, shower and a conveniently central location. It was less than a ten-minute walk away from Beale Street, the famed Black entertainment (jazz and nightclub) and dining district in Memphis. In fact, its proximity to Beale Street turned the Lorraine Motel into a preferred stop for a wide array of touring artists. Jazz great Count Basie stayed there and, later, Gospel and Rhythm & Blues singer Aretha Franklin. The motel catered to more than celebrities. It also was available to the everyday traveller. It was prominently featured in *The Negro Motorist Green Book* (commonly called the *Green Book*), which listed comfortable and, more importantly safe, lodgings that were open and welcoming to African American guests during an era of extreme segregation and a proliferation of 'Whites Only' hotels.

The Lorraine Motel began as a racially restricted ('Whites Only') establishment in the 1920s. Originally built as a one-level hotel (the Windsor Hotel), it was renovated with the construction of a second level replete with an open-air walkway/balcony that enabled access to its newly constructed rooms.[11] Reopened as a 'motel', a relatively new lodging concept – blending 'motor' and 'hotel' – the establishment was designed to appeal to the annually increasingly waves of car travellers and tourists. In 1945, it was sold to Walter and Loree Bailey, African American entrepreneurs, who enthusiastically opened their doors to Black travellers while reserving a separate wing exclusively available to white guests (and conforming with segregationist laws of the 1940 and 1950s).

When Martin Luther King, Jr., began to crisscross the United States in support of civil rights, the city of Memphis was a frequent stop in his circuit. The city boasted a vibrant African American community who demonstrably contributed to the emergent culture of the state. Although a southern city, there were more progressive elements to be found there than elsewhere in the United States, in contrast to the more frequently explicit racisms of Mississippi or the more covert (but equally insidious) prejudice of Illinois. In addition, the Black community in Memphis shaped everyday life in the city. Not only did African American workers provide vital services, the Black community, through the cultural offerings of Beale Street, existed as an enviable showcase of Black excellence, sophistication and leisure. Elvis Presley, the white rock-n-roll artist who is arguably the most famous resident of Memphis, derived his sound by emulating the music of Beale Street artists.

In addition to its location, the Lorraine Motel had several other features that appealed to King. As a motor lodge, it granted easy and quick access to bedrooms. Simply park your car in the lot below, walk up the outdoor stairs to the second floor (where King stayed) and open the door to your room. There were no lobbies to walk through or elevators for which to wait. Its efficiency appealed to the weary guest eager for quiet and rest. A cigarette smoker, King also enjoyed the opportunity to walk outside his room, stand on his balcony and survey the activity below as he smoked. Indeed, his tendency to loiter on the balcony and talk with advisers was well known to supporters, who would sometimes assemble below to catch a glimpse of the civil rights leaders. Unfortunately, it was also known to his detractors and those who sought to harm him.

Following King's' assassination, the Lorraine Motel would continue to operate as a lodging establishment even as the place eventually became recognizable as a memorial. People wanted to visit the last place where King stood and remember both the man and his legacy. In time, the Lorraine Motel would become a formal museum, the National Civil Rights Museum. Today, the museum is among the most popular historical sites in Memphis, with an overall visitorship in the millions. It is estimated that nearly 90,000 students visit every year.[12] The feel of the 1960s has been preserved. Vintage cars are parked in the lot below the balcony where King was shot. Marking the place of King, a white wreath hangs on the railing near where he collapsed after being struck by the gunman's bullet. It invites the visitor to look up, imagine King and remember the violence that ended his life.

Inside King's motel room, the space has been preserved almost as if time stopped on that fateful day. Two beds appear with one undisturbed and the other, presumably King's, showing the slightest signs that it had been slept in. The orange blanket and white sheet are slightly pulled back to reveal one of the bed's two pillows, giving the impression that Martin Luther King, Jr., rested his head there. A newspaper sits on the other bed. A breakfast tray with coffee and elsewhere another cup of coffee adjacent to a carton of milk offer the sense of King's morning ritual. We get a glimpse of how the civil rights leader started his day. The normalcy of the ritual and non-luxurious setting of the space of the hotel room can have a profound impact on the visitor. The scale of the tragedy seems out of proportion to this rather normal and frankly underwhelming space.

However, it was here that an act occurred that would compromise the Civil Rights Movement and bring about global mourning. The room helps us to remember that Martin Luther King, Jr., was not a mythological titan but rather a person, an individual. He needed sleep. He smoked cigarettes. An ashtray with nearly a dozen cigarette butts suggests that King, who preferred not to be photographed smoking, was a habitual smoker. Like everyone, he needed to make use of a bathroom – and the small, cramped and well-preserved motel room bathroom includes King's toiletry case. The motel room gives a human scale to Martin Luther King, Jr., and helps us to appreciate the potential that we all possess to bring about major change.

Theatre and human rights

For nearly two centuries, theatre has served as the repository of African American culture, history and memory. Second only to music (and song), it is the medium of expression that has been essential to recording the past – experiences and hopes – for present and future generations. The centrality of theatre in the transmission of history can be attributed to two elements. First, it evidences the maintenance of an Africanist oral storytelling tradition. Most commonly represented by a griot, a storyteller (in Yoruban culture), this narrative form enabled a nomadic people to move and travel without losing ties to history. Standing before other townsfolk, the griot would speak of the ancestors, allowing their past achievements to be heard and remembered by their descendants. Being a highly skilled performer who was trained to be the keeper of memories for a society, the griot was an essential member of the community. Second, the centrality of theatre emerges as a result of the experience of chattel slavery and discrimination within the United States. African captives were prohibited from learning how to read – and tortured (and, sometimes, killed) for the pursuit of literacy. As a result, the relay of culture had to occur primarily through non-written means: song and storytelling.

Although the first professional Black theatre company in the United States is considered to be the African Theatre (or African

Grove) in New York City in 1821, the movement to consistently represent African American culture would not occur until the end of the century. As a nascent theatre industry was developing within the country, the stage was deployed to offer an insight into various aspects of Black life and to campaign against racist practices. The cause of abolition, the effort to end slavery, utilized the art form of drama. Among the earliest performances were accounts of dramatic escapes from slavery. Henry Box Brown and Ellen Craft (alongside her husband William) captivated late nineteenth-century audiences by telling and performing how they fled to freedom. Brown hid in a box and, as cargo, shipped himself to a non-slave state. Craft passed as a white man (with her darker-complexioned husband pretending to be her slave) and travelled northward away from the slave-holding American South. Although audiences certainly were captivated by the drama of the escapes, they could not have missed the abolitionist sentiment that rested at its core.

The movement towards civil rights and social revolution was supported by theatre makers. At the turn of the twentieth century, theatre, which was the most popular form of entertainment before the advent of film, television and radio, existed as a significant medium to advance the cause of social equality. Sociologist W. E. B. Du Bois called for artists to create theatre to not only challenge stereotypes but also confront racial discrimination. Through his advocacy and, more specifically, because of the support provided by his magazine *The Crisis* alongside upstart theatre companies, such as the Harlem-based Krigwa Players in 1926, a politically engaged theatre emerged that directly addressed lynchings, discrimination and segregation. Prominent playwrights to emerge during this period include Angelina Weld Grimké and Marita Bonner.

The work of theatre to mirror society and to advance the cause of civil rights would continue. James Baldwin's *Blues for Mister Charlie* (1964) offers a story inspired by the murder of Emmett Till. In *A Raisin in the Sun* (1959), Lorraine Hansberry focuses on the problems of housing discrimination. In Douglas Turner Ward's *Day of Absence* (1965), the playwright attempts to demonstrate how essential Black and African American citizens are to every aspect of society by imagining a day in which all Black folk disappeared. Amiri Baraka's *Dutchman* (1964) pushed the social commentary of theatre by noting that the stage needs not only to document discrimination but also to call for revolution. In the play, the character Clay, a college-aged man, is harassed on the subway by a white woman who berates him and eventually kills him. The lesson is that societal racism literally runs deep (to the depths of the underground subway lines) and can target you anywhere. Not only vigilance but also revolution is necessary to overthrow the supremacist culture that targets Black children, women and men.

Although theatre may not drive the national conversation in the same manner that it did a century ago, the stage and the invitation to gather and co-witness a live performance offers an unparalleled opportunity to collectively look upon our society. In recent decades, theatrical productions have continued to offer a lens into the ongoing need to address societal inequities as evidenced in the dramas of Suzan-Lori Parks, Dominique Morisseau, Lynn Nottage and Katori Hall among others. These plays alongside the conversations that they engender among audiences as they exit the auditorium (or participate in reading group or post-performance discussions) serve as necessary prompts to continue the work of social justice and inclusion. Certainly, one of the questions that *The Mountaintop* asks us is how we can continue the work and champion the legacy of Martin Luther King, Jr.

Imagining history

Raised in Memphis, Tennessee, playwright Katori Hall was acquainted with the Lorraine Motel. She remembers, 'My mother grew up one block away.'[13] As a child, Hall was often told stories about how her mother, Carrie Mae, *almost* saw Martin Luther King, Jr., on the eve of his death. Carrie Mae had wanted to see King speak at Mason Temple. However, Hall's grandmother prohibited her daughter from going to the event. She was worried that the church would be bombed. There had been death threats. Not only was King's life in jeopardy but so too were the lives of anyone in close physical proximity to the preacher. Indeed, King himself seemed well aware of his own mortality and, that day, would speak of a premonition concerning his death. Not seeing King would be the 'greatest regret of my mother's life', Hall recalled.[14] Referring to her play, Hall observed, 'I wanted to put both of them in the same room and give my mother that opportunity that she didn't have in 1968'.[15] Camae (an abridging of Carrie Mae) would meet the civil rights leader in *The Mountaintop*.

Katori Hall studied African American studies as an undergraduate college student at Columbia University before completing graduate work in acting at Harvard University. After Harvard, she studied playwriting at the Juilliard School. It would be as a Juilliard student that she would begin drafting *The Mountaintop*. The play reflects her early college and university explorations. It spotlights an important time period and figure in American history (and, by extension, African American studies). Katori Hall researched Martin Luther King, Jr., before writing the play. Although *The Mountaintop* is certainly a work of fiction, the playwright incorporates many aspects of fact from his life. She states,

> A lot of people are not privy to this, but King was quite depressed those last few months of his life. He had taken up smoking to deal with the mounting stress and responsibilities of leading a movement. He was heavily criticized for leading a garbage strikers march in Memphis that had unfortunately turned violent, a young 16-year-old boy named Larry Payne was killed. He was deeply troubled in a way his colleagues had never seen him after that. He came back to Memphis . . . for the garbage strike workers because their quest for a living wage paralleled his quest for a living wage for all Americans.[16]

Committed to presenting the civil rights leader as an individual and not a mythic (and therefore unrelatable) icon, Hall commits to showcasing King's humanity. According to Hall, this 'warts-and-all portrayal of Dr. King is important because there's this extraordinary human being who is actually quite ordinary'.[17] However, the ordinariness of King should not be misconstrued as a critique of the influential leader. Hall offers, 'I feel as though by portraying him with his flaws and foibles, we, too, can see – as human beings who have these flaws – that we, too, can be Kings; we, too, can carry on that baton that he has passed down to us.'[18]

A signature element of Katori Hall's playwriting is the creation of characters with whom it is easy to find a connection through their seeming realness. Her experience as a performer enabled her to appreciate the need for more roles for Black actors, especially Black women. In a 2012 interview, Hall discloses, 'I started out as an actress and . . . [was] so frustrated. I was frustrated that there wasn't anything . . . for me to play and step into the shoes of'.[19] In one oft-cited story from her acting studies, she remembers a class assignment in which students were divided into pairs and told to find a scene from a play for them to rehearse and perform. Paired with another Black actress, Hall and her partner struggled to find a scene featuring two Black women. Although there is a small but compelling literature penned by Black women playwrights featuring Black women characters, Hall realized the need to create more opportunities for Black actors and the necessity of better amplifying the literature that currently exists.

The Mountaintop was the first of Hall's theatrical works to attract widespread popular attention. It was produced in London in 2009 and quickly transferred to the West End. A critical success, Hall was hailed as an important, emerging voice in the theatre. The play won both an Olivier Award (London) for Best New Play and the Pulitzer Prize in Drama. A Broadway production, starring Samuel L. Jackson and Angela Bassett, soon followed. Later, Hall would adapt the biography of singer Tina Turner for the stage in *I, Tina* (2018). That play tells the story of Ida Mae Bullock, a young southern woman and her experiences with poverty, sexism, racism and domestic abuse, en route to becoming one of the world's most famous musical artists. Similar to *The Mountaintop*, Hall focuses on the person and reveals the challenges faced by Tina Turner. Katori Hall also has written for television, such as *P-Valley* (2020–22), which was based on one of her plays and features women who work in a southern strip club. Reflecting on her ability to create stage and screen works that feature Black women as 'soul quenching in the best way', Hall notes, 'I'm just so grateful that I've been able to contribute, whether it's to the stage, to TV and hopefully one day to film, a different shade of what it means to be a Black woman in America, particularly a Black woman growing up in the American south'.[20]

Staging the mountain

The Mountaintop is the type of play that theatre artists describe as a 'two-hander'. It involves only two actors. Although this format is quite popular for shorter works, such as ten-minute plays and one-acts, it is a complicated endeavour for a full-length play. The weight of the drama is borne by only two people who have the responsibility to maintain the momentum of the narrative and to keep the audience engaged. To appreciate the rigour of a 'two-hander', it is helpful to remember that most plays do not have this structure. Think about your favourite play. How long does it take for the playwright to introduce a third person? Often, the third (or fourth) character arrives pretty quickly. Although there are phone calls (such as to Coretta Scott King) and announcements to offstage characters (such as to Ralph Abernathy) in *The Mountaintop*, only two characters – Martin Luther King, Jr., and Camae – are present onstage.

All of the action of the play takes place in King's room, Room 306, at the Lorraine Motel on 3 April 1968, the evening before Martin Luther King, Jr.'s assassination. King has recently returned from Mason Temple. Filled with both energy from the audience response and a sense of foreboding, he is restless. He paces. He smokes cigarettes. He needs to be in conversation with someone and, fortunately, Camae, initially described by Katori Hall as a 'beautiful young maid', enters. What ensues is an engaging and, occasionally, flirtatious conversation which touches on a range of topics mostly revolving around the movement for civil rights. Slowly, it becomes apparent that Camae is more than she appears to be. Arriving with the next day's newspaper and knowledgeable about King's boyhood past (and his original birth name), she possesses an authority that ultimately shifts the balance between the two. Whereas the play begins with King as the powerful character, it ends with Camae, a recently appointed angel tasked with preparing King for his death, controlling the narrative.

Camae is a complex character whose multidimensionality enables Katori Hall to reveal different aspects of Martin Luther King, Jr. Whereas the playwright could have chosen to introduce the angel in a resplendent manner, the understated entrance of Camae as a motel employee gives the narrative room to grow (25). Indeed, the slow reveal of Camae's true identity helps to keep audiences engaged with the two-hander. Clues are introduced that help audiences understand that Camae is more than she seems. Indeed, at one moment, she confesses, 'I ain't your ordinary ole maid' (44). When King asks, 'How'd yall get tomorrow's paper?', Camae's physical response is more telling than her words. She 'shrugs' (35). To an audience aware of King's looming assassination, Camae provides the foreshadowing. Referring to lightning and thunderclaps, whose sonic boom resembles a gunshot, she tells King, 'God'll strike you down if you move 'round too much' (27). Later, in reference to cigarettes, she declares, 'Civil rights'll kill ya fo' Pall Malls will' (36). She notes that 'God ain't gone stop cryin' no time soon' (39) and tells King that he will see Malcolm in heaven 'One day' (47). Indeed, he will die in one day.

In the opening moments of the play, Hall offers her audience a representation of Martin Luther King, Jr., as an everyday person with common needs and vices. His first words are a request for cigarettes. He speaks in a short, clipped phrases, which contrasts with the popular memory of the loftier and grander eloquence of King the orator. Among his first actions is going to the bathroom. We hear him urinate and flush a toilet. He smells his shoes and comments on foot odour. Indeed, a lot happens in the few minutes to establish Martin Luther King, Jr., the character in *The Mountaintop*, as different than (and unlike) the mythic figure recorded and captured in American history. This is not the King who resides in our imagination. Although a more realistic depiction of the icon, it actually serves as a reminder that the play itself is a work of fiction.

The humanity of King is essential to the 'two-hander' structure of the play. It renders him multidimensional and, therefore, provides more opportunities to explore aspects of the character. King, as written by Hall, exists as a series of contradictory impulses, which itself is a sign of his deep humanity. He is both flirtatious with Camae and protective of his wife, Coretta Scott King. He pivots between colloquial, everyday speech and the lofty, poetic rhetoric, for which he is most often remembered. In time, his façade of indomitable confidence in the face of death threats shatters. King reveals his fears and concerns about his own mortality. In these ways, the civil rights icon as a protagonist within a play becomes more relatable. Our awareness of King as a plainly human individual with faults and worries enables our identification with the character and ensures that his legacy (and memory) will be championed by future generations.

The Mountaintop is fundamentally not about a legendary leader who climbed a mountain in an effort to overcome prejudice and racism. Yes, Martin Luther King, Jr., is the protagonist of the story. The centring of the narrative on the eve of his assassination creates the sense that the play is about him. However, this attention on King as a man and not a myth gifts audiences (and readers) with an understanding of their own capacity to create change in the world. The play is about our ability to transform society. If King could summit the mountain, then it is possible for others – for us – to do the same. King, in *The Mountaintop*, tells us, we 'are the climbers, the new carriers of the cross'.

Notes

1 'Martin Luther King's "I Have a Dream" Speech in Its Entirety', *NPR Talk of the Nation*, 16 January 2023. https://www.npr.org/2010/01/18 /122701268/i-have-a-dream-speech-in-its-entirety

2 Derek H. Alderman, 'School Names as Cultural Arenas: The Naming of U.S. Public Schools after Martin Luther King, Jr', *Urban Geography*, 23, no. 7 (2002): 601–26. DOI: 10.2747/0272-3638.23.7.601

3 Clarissa Myrick-Harris, 'The Origins of the Civil Rights Movement in Atlanta, 1880-1910', *Perspectives on History*, 1 November 2006. https:// www.historians.org/research-and-publications/perspectives-on-history /november-2006/the-origins-of-the-civil-rights-movement-in-atlanta -1880-1910

4 'King, Martin Luther, Sr'. *King Encyclopedia*. The Martin Luther King, Jr Research and Education Institute. https://kinginstitute.stanford.edu/ encyclopedia

5 Jason Oliver Evans, 'How Ebenezer Baptist Church Has Been a Seat of Black Power for Generations', *The Conversation*, 15 January 2021.

6 Martin Luther King, Jr, 'Letter from Birmingham Jail', August 1963. https://www.csuchico.edu/iege/_assets/documents/susi-letter-from -birmingham-jail.pdf

7 Martin Luther King, Jr, *The Autobiography of Martin Luther King, Jr.*, ed. Claybourne Carson (New York: Warner Books, 1998).

8   Ibid.

9   Ibid.

10 King, 'I've Been to the Mountaintop', Address Delivered at Bishop
    Charles Mason Temple, in *A Call to Conscience*, ed. Clayborne Carson
    and Kris Shepard (New York: Grand Central Publishing, 2001).

11 Allyson Hobbs, 'The Lorraine Motel and Martin Luther King', *The New
    Yorker*, 18 January 2016.

12 'The National Civil Rights Museum at the Lorraine Motel Reopens
    March 1', National Civil Rights Museum, 18 February 2021. https://
    www.globenewswire.com/en/news-release/2021/02/18/2178368/0/en
    /The-National-Civil-Rights-Museum-at-the-Lorraine-Motel-Reopens
    -March-1.html

13 Playwrights Foundation, 'Interview with Katori Hall', 18 April 2008.
    https://playwrightsfoundation.org/2008/04/18/interview-with-katori
    -hall-2/

14 Ibid.

15 'Broadway to Get a View from MLK's "Mountaintop"', *NPR All Things
    Considered*, 31 March 2011.

16 Playwrights Foundation.

17 'Broadway'.

18 Ibid.

19 Carolyn M. Brown, 'Playwright Katori Hall Celebrates MLK's Legacy
    with "The Mountaintop"', *Black Enterprise*, 2 January 2012. https://www
    .blackenterprise.com/mountaintop-katori-hall-on-martin-luther-king
    -jr-legacy/

20 Tyler Doster, 'Katori Hall on Her Pulitzer, Adapting Her Own Work
    and Hiring an All-Women Team for Season Two of "P-Valley"',
    Awardswatch, 23 June 2021. https://awardswatch.com/interview-katori
    -hall-on-her-pulitzer-adapting-her-own-work-and-hiring-an-all
    -women-team-for-season-two-of-p-valley/

The Mountaintop

The Mountaintop was developed during the Lark Play Development Center Barebones workshop in New York City on 29 April 2009 (John Eisner, artistic director; Michael Roberston, man- ageing director). The cast was as follows:

Dr Martin Luther King, Jr.   Jordan Mahome
Camae   Dominique Morisseau
Directed by Kamilah Forbes
Stage Manager Stacy Waring

The Mountaintop had its world premiere at Theatre 503, London, on 9 June 2009 (Tim Roseman and Paul Robinson, artistic directors). The cast was as follows:

Dr Martin Luther King, Jr.   David Harewood
Camae   Lorraine Burroughs
Directed by James Dacre
Set and costume design by Libby Watson
Lighting design by Emma Chapman
Music and sound by Richard Hammarton
Video design by Dick Straker for Mesmer
Line producer Davina Shah

This production transferred to Trafalgar Studios, West End, on 21 July 2009 (produced by Sonia Friedman Productions, Jean Doumanian, Tali Pelman for Ambassador Theatre Group, Bob Bartner, Freddy DeMan, Jerry Frankel, Ted Snowdon and Marla Rubin Productions Ltd).

The Mountaintop opened at the Bernard B. Jacobs Theatre on Broadway in New York City on 13 October 2011 (Produced by Jean Doumanian, Sonia Friedman, Ambassador Theatre Group, Tali Pelman, Ted Snowdon, Raise the Roof 7, Alhadeff Productions/Lauren Doll, B Square + 4 Productions/ Broadway Across America, Jacki Barlia Florin/Cooper Federman, Ronnie Planalp/Moellenberg Taylor, Marla Rubin Productions/Blumenthal Performing Arts). The cast was as follows:

Dr Martin Luther King, Jr.   Samuel L. Jackson
Camae   Angela Bassett

Directed by Kenny Leon
Set and video design by David Gallo
Costume design by Constanza Romero
Lighting design by Brian MacDevitt
Sound design by Dan Moses Schreier
Music composition by Branford Marsalis

Characters

Dr. Martin Luther King, Jr.   Thirty-nine, Nobel Peace Prize-winning Civil Rights Movement leader.

Camae   Twenties, Lorraine Motel maid.

Setting

3 April 1968.
Room 306, Lorraine Motel, Memphis, Tennessee.

Lights up. Night. 3 April 1968. Room 306, the Lorraine Motel, Memphis, Tennessee. The outside street lights project the shadows of rain sliding down the pane on to the walls.

The motel room door creaks open. The rain pours outside. Enter **Dr. Martin Luther King, Jr**. *Tired. Overwrought. Wet. He is ready to take his shoes off and crawl into bed. He coughs. He is hoarse. He stands in the doorway, the red and yellow motel sign casting a glow on to his face. He yells out of the door into the stormy night.*

King   Abernathy, get me a pack of Pall Malls, when ya go. Naw. Naw. Naw. I said Pall Malls. I don't like those Winstons you smoke. You can call me siddity all you like, I want me a Pall Mall. Pall Malls, man! Don't be cheap. Be back soon, man. I'm wanting one. Bad. That's right . . . That's right . . .

He closes the door. He locks the deadbolt. Click. He chains the door. Rattle. Then he pulls the curtain tight over the window. He walks around in the darkness, but he knows the lay of the room well. He turns on a lone lamp that instantly illuminates the room. Water stains pockmark the walls. Bright orange and fading brown sixties decor accent the room. The carpet is the color of bile. He loosens his tie. Unbuttons his shirt. Coughs.

An opened briefcase lies on one of the two full beds, covered with rumpled peach sheets. He picks up his sermon papers from the bed.

(*Reading.*) 'Why America is going to Hell . . . '

He goes into the bathroom.

'Why America is going to Hell . . . '

We hear him urinate. He flushes the toilet. He walks back into the room.

They really gonna burn me on the cross for that one.

'America, you are too ARROGANT!'

He goes to the nightstand and checks the empty coffee cups.

What shall I say . . . what shall I say . . .

He goes to the black rotary phone on the night stand between the beds. He dials.

America . . . Ameri –

He stops. In complete silence: unscrews the receiver. Checks the phone for bugs. None there. Screws the receiver back. Checks the night stand. None there. Sighs. Dials again.

Room service? There's not any more room service, tonight? When did it stop? Last week? We were here last week and y'all were still serving room service till midnight. Been always able to get me a cup of coffee when I wanted it. Needed it. Pardon? I just want a coffee. One cup. (*Pause.*) Thank you! Got to do some work before I go to bed. You can bring it on up. Room 306. (*He smiles a broad smile.*) Yes, we call it the 'King-Abernathy Suite' too. I appreciate that, sir. We thank you for your prayers, sir. We're not gonna stop. These sanitation workers gonna get their due. I'm here to make sure of that. Yes, sir! My autograph, sir? (*Beat.*) Uhhh . . . I don't give those out. I only give thanks. Sorry, sir. Yes. It'll be right up? Five minutes? Thank you kindly. Kindly.

He hangs up. He gives the phone a 'what the fuck was that about' look.

'America, America, my country 'tis of thee . . . '

He begins to take off his shoes.

'My country who doles out constant misery – '

He smells them.

Wooooh! Sweet Jesus. I got marching feet and we ain't even marched yet!

He throws them down. He turns to rifle through his suitcase.

Shit. She forgot to pack my toothbrush again.

He dials on the rotary phone.

(*Singing to himself.*) Corrie, pick up . . . Corrie pick up, Corrie, Corrie, Corrie, pick up . . .

She doesn't. He puts the phone down.

My country who doles out constant misery. War abroad. Then war in your streets. (*Under his breath.*) 'Arrogant America.' What shall I do with bbbbbb –

He throws himself back on the bed. There is a knock at the door. He rushes to go and answer. He undoes the deadbolt, then the chain.

Reverend, about time, man. The store ain't but down the street –

Enter **Camae***, a beautiful young maid. She stands in the doorway, one hand holding a newspaper over her head to catch the rain, the other balancing a tray with a cup of coffee.*

Camae   Room service, sir.

King   That was fast.

Camae   Well, I been called Quickie Camae befo'.

He is taken aback, stunned by her beauty. She waits and waits and waits. He snaps out of it.

King   Where are my manners? Come on in.

He steps aside. She walks in. Dripping over everything.

Camae   Where would you like me to put this?

King   On the table over there.

She sets the tray on the downstage table, bending slightly at the waist. **King** *appreciates his view. Beat. She looks back; he looks away.*

King   How much is that gonna cost?

Camae   Folk down there say it's on the house. For you. It like this yo' house, they say. So you ain't gotta pay them. But you *can* pay me a tip for gettin' my press 'n curl wet out in this rain.

She holds out her hand. He smiles and pulls money from his billfold.

King   You new?

Camae   First day, sir.

King   That's why. I haven't seen you before. Stayed here plenty a' times, but I've never seen your face.

Camae   I done seen yo's befo' though.

King   Oh, have you?

Camae   Of course. On the TV down at Woolworth's. You like the Beatles.

King   Wish folks would listen to me like they listen to the Beatles.

Camae   Mmhm. 'Specially white folks.

King *laughs, then breaks into a fit of coughs.*

Camae   Sound like you needin' some tea, not no coffee. You got a cold?

King (*straining*)   Just done got to getting hoarse. Shouting.

Camae   And carryin' on.

King   No, not carrying on. Testifying.

Camae   Shame I ain't get a chance to see ya tonight. I heard you carried on a storm up at Mason Temple.

King   How you know?

Camae   Negro talk strike faster than lightnin'. They say folks was all cryin'. Sangin'. Mmph. Mmph. Mmph. I woulda liked to have seen that. Somethin' to tell my chiren. 'When I wun't nothin' but a chick-a-dee, I seen't Dr. Martin Luther Kang, Jr cuttin' up in the pulpit.' Mmmhmm. I bet that was somethin' to see.

King *goes to peek out of the window.*

King   Wish it had been more folks there.

Camae   How many was there?

King   Mmmm. A couple thousand.

Camae   Honey, that a lot.

King   Coulda been more in my humble opinion.

Camae   But it was stormin'. Tornadoes and all get out. You can't get no Negro folks out in no rain like this.

King   And why is that?

Camae   God'll strike you down if you move 'round too much. That what my momma used to say. When it storm like this my momma'd say, "Be still!" But I thank she just wanted us chiren to sit our tails down somewhere 'cause the lightnin' spooked her nerves so bad. Personally, I just thank God be actin' up.

King   Do He? Is that why *you* didn't come?

Pause. She wants to say something, but changes her mind.

Camae   Naw. It my first day here. At work. Wanted to come in early.

King   Well, I can't blame folks. Shoot, *I* almost didn't go.

Camae   Why that?

King   Ain't been feeling too good.

Camae   Aww, a little sick?

King   You could say that . . . Personally, I don't think God's what kept folks in their houses tonight. Folks just don't care.

Camae   Folks 'fraid of gettin' blown up. Churches ain't even safe for us folks.

Thunder and lightning. Boom. Boom. Crackle! **King** *jumps slightly.*

Camae   You . . . all right?

King (*fidgeting*)   Sure . . . sure.

Beat. She goes stage left, checks the bathroom. Takes some wet towels out and slings them across her shoulder.

Camae   You need anythang else 'fore I go?

King   Actually . . . if you got a cigarette . . .

Camae   Cigarettes *and* coffee? That ain't a diet befittin' of a preacher.

King   'Judge not and ye shall not be judged.'

Camae   Honey, I hears that. I guess if you was at home you'd be eatin' mo' right.

King   I suppose.

Camae   What you miss the most she make?

King   Her egg sandwiches.

Camae   Mmm. I likes them, too. Make one every day for myself.

She pulls out a pack of cigarettes. Offers him one. He takes it gladly. Looks at it closely. Staring her down, he puts it in his mouth. She takes out a lighter. Lights it for him.

King   Not too many women running 'round smoking Pall Malls. Impressive.

Camae   Quite. My daddy smoked Pall Malls. Said Kools'll kill ya.

King   Have yourself one.

Camae   What?

King   Smoke one with me.

Camae (*smiling*)   Naw, naw, Preacher Kang. You 'bout to have my boss up after me. I don't know what the rules is yet. Don't know where the dark corners in this place is to hide and smoke my Pall Malls. Don't even know which rooms to lay my head for a quick nap.

King   What about this one?

Beat. She looks at the bed.

Camae   Last folk up in here was doin' the hoochie coochie for pay. I wouldn't lay down in that bed if somebody paid me.

King   So what kinds of rules does a little lady like you break?

Camae   None that involve no preacher, I tells ya that.

King   Everybody should break a rule every now and then.

Camae   Yessir. I's agrees witcha. But not tonight . . . *Not* tonight.

King   Have one wit' me. They're not gonna come looking for you.

Camae (*laughing nervously*)   You the one gone get caught. Kidnappin' me like this.

King   Just one. Till my friend come back with my pack.

Beat. She sighs. She takes a cigarette out and lights it. Inhales. Lets it all out. They look at each other.

Camae   You sho'll do try hard at it.

King   Well . . . you're pretty.

Camae   I know. Even my uncle couldn't help hisself. You have fun tonight?

King   Fun?

Camae   It gotta be fun. Otherwise you wouldn't do it.

King   Not any fun in this.

Camae   Sound like grand fun to me. Standin' up there in the middle of them great big old churches. People clappin' for you. Fallin' out. (*To herself.*) Must be muthafuckin' grand to mean so much to somebody. Shit, *goddamn* must be grand. (*Beat.*) Where a needle and thread to sew up my mouth? Here I is just a' cussin' all up in front of you, Dr. Kang. I cuss worser than a sailor with the clap. Oooo, God gone get me!

I'm goin' to hell just for cussin' in front of you. Fallin' straight to hell.

He laughs.

King   No ma'am, 'cordin' to your face, you done fell straight from heaven.

He sips his coffee.

Camae   You lil' pulpit poet you. I likes you.

King   I 'likes' you, too.

The phone rings.

Excuse me.

Camae   Well, I'll just be on my –

*He motions for her to stay. Then puts on his '**King** voice'.*

King   Dr. King, here. (*Voice shifts.*) Oh, Corrie. Yes. I did call. You didn't pick up. Oh. You were at a meeting. Oh. It went fine. Not as many people there, but . . . it was enough. I am getting hoarse, I know. Yes, I'm drinking my tea. I'm drinking tea right now.

He looks at **Camae***, who snickers. He motions for her to be quiet.*

King   You know you forgot to pack my toothbrush? Yeap.

He laughs, checks his breath.

I'll just get another one in the morning. Don't worry, darling. You can't remember everything. (*Silence.*) Did they call? What they say this time? Hmm. Hmm. Ugly voices. Mmph. You worried? I'm not.

He takes a long drag on his cigarette.

The children asleep? Oh. *She* still up. She shouldn't be up so late past midnight. Oh, she can't sleep. Well, let me talk to her. (*Pause.*) Hey, it's Paw. Mmmhmm. What Paw say? You have to listen to your Ma when Paw's not there. Yes. You having trouble sleeping? Me too, sometime. You know what in no time. It makes everything real peaceful. You promise you gonna be good? Okay, let Paw speak to your Ma. Oh. She's in the bathroom, now? Just tell Yolanda and the boys Paw'll see 'em when I get back. Tell Ma I love her. Goodnight, Bernice.

He hangs up the phone.

Camae   You shouldn't lie like that.

King   Like what?

Camae   About drankin' tea. Lyin' tail.

King   Coffee can't cure a cold, can it?

Camae   Coffee wit' some whiskey in it can.

She pulls out a flask and casts a dollop into his cup.

This what the Irish call 'cough syrup'.

King *laughs heartily.*

Camae   She's beautiful. Yo' wife. I seen't her on the TV down at Woolworth's, too. Corretta Scott K –

King (*correcting*)   *Mrs.* King.

Camae   Oh. Yes. *Mrs.* King.

He drinks his coffee.

King   The color of coffee with a lot of milk and a lot of sugar. Just how I like it.

Camae   Well, I likes my coffee black and bitter.

He looks at the name tag on her chest.

King   'Carrie Mae'. That's not what you said earlier.

Camae   Folk shorten it. Call me Camae.

King   Carriemae?

Camae   Naw, naw, na! CA–MAE. Camae.

King   Doesn't make any sense.

Camae   It do too. Say it wit' me. (*Slowly.*) Camae.

King   Cammmae.

Camae   Camae!

King (*teasing*)   CAR–mae?

Camae   CAMAE!

King (*laughing*)   Camae!

Camae (*laughing too*)   Right! Right! There ya go. Sound good comin' outcho mouth.

King   A lot of things do.

Camae   Sho'll do.

King   Sho'll do.

Beat.

Camae   Well, you axe for me if you need anythang else. Just pick up the phone and give me a hollah. The switchboard man'll get me.

King   I can ask for you especially?

Camae   If me is what you want.

Beat.

King   Alrighty then.

Camae   Alrighty then.

She slowly makes her way to the door. She looks back to him. Smiles. She opens the door. The storm has gathered more fury outside. BOOM, BOOM. BOOM!!

King (*stuttering*)   C-c-can I ask you a question before you go? And you promise to answer me open and honest?

Camae   Depend on what the question is.

King   You won't think me less of a man, if I ask?

Camae   I might.

King I've been needing a woman's perspective on this.

Camae Like I say, it depend on the question. Shoot.

She closes the door. Beat.

King Do you think I should shave off my mustache?

Beat.

Camae Yes. I was just sayin' that to myself just then, 'He look so damn ugly with that mustache.'

King Really?

Camae Naw! I thought you was gone ask me about somethin' mo' important than that.

King That is important! My physical appearance is important. To the people.

Camae Gone on somewhere wit' that!

King I'm serious! Tell me the truth. Mustache, no mustache?

He covers his mustache with his hand, then uncovers and covers again.

Mustache or no mustache? Mustache or no mustache?

Camae (*laughing*) Where is that man witcho Pall Malls so you can stop axin' me crazy questions?

King I don't know where Ralph is. I just thought I'd get a woman's opinion.

Camae Well, have you axed yo' wife?

Beat.

King No.

Camae Well, axe her then. She the one supposed to make them kinds of decisions anyway.

King *goes to the mirror downstage and peers at his face.*

King Just tryin' to shave some years off. I done got to looking old.

Camae   You have. You look older. In person. When women get older, they get ugly. When men get older they get . . . handsome. Wrinkles look good on a man. Especially when they got some money to go wit' they wrinkles.

King   Women do like men with wrinkles, don't they?

Camae   I don't. I likes 'em young and wild. Like me.

King   Like you?

Camae   Yes, Preacher Kang.

King (*smiling at the memory*)   I used to be young and wild myself.

Camae   You a preacher. That's part a' y'all job requirement. How you know what you ain't supposed to do if you ain't done it, yaself ? Folk won't listen to you otherwise. That what I call 'work experience'. More than qualify ya for the position.

King   And what qualify you to be a maid?

Camae   I'm betta at cleanin' up other folks' messes than my own. I was called to do this.

King   Well. I think I was, too.

He sees that his cigarette is finished.

Can I have another one?

Camae   You ain't gone leave me here to work through the night wit nothin' to smoke on. Shhhh-iiii – oooot! All I got is one square left.

King   Perhaps we can share?

He moves closer to her. Beat.

Camae   Like, I say, you *sho'll* try hard at it.

He holds his hand out.

King   Well, the spirit is willing, but the flesh is weak.

As she speaks the following, she hands him her last cigarette. Lights it for him. Then throws her empty pack into the trash can.

Camae   Mmph, mmph, *mmph*! These goddamn folk got you chain smokin' harder than a muthafucka.

Beat.

There I go! Got to cussin' again. I am so sorry, Preacher Kang. I am *so sorry*. I should be shamed of myself. God gone get me for that one, too.

King   Don't worry. I forgive you.

Camae   I'm glad somebody do.

They look at each other softly.

King   Well, I guess you got other folks' messes to clean up . . . I don't mean to keep ya. Don't forget your umbrella.

He hands her the wet newspaper she had brought in.

Camae   Unh, unh. That ain't mine. Thass yours. Boss told me to bring that up for you. Sorry, I got it wet.

King   Well, I thank ya. Thank ya kindly.

He looks at the newspaper.

April 4th? How'd y'all get tomorrow's paper?

Camae (*shrugs*)   Tomorrow already here.

King (*reads*)   'King Challenges Court Restraint. Vows to March' – they got that right! This Mayor Loeb calls himself not allowing these sanitation workers to march. (*To himself.*) Over my dead body. 'Yesterday two US marshalls sped across town to serve the Negro leaders with copies of the order. They found Dr. King and four other defendants at the Lorraine Motel . . . ' (*He reads further and further.*)

Camae   Folks can send you flowers. Since they know where you stayin'.

King   That ain't the only thing they can send me. (*Reads.*) 'The

city said it was seeking the injunction as a means of protecting
Dr. King . . . We are fearful that in the turmoil of the moment,
someone may even harm Dr. King's life . . . and with all the force
of language we can use, we want to emphasize that we don't
want that to happen . . .' (*Chuckles to himself.*) Wish the mayor
had jurisdiction over airplanes, too. You know, Camae, somebody
called in a bomb threat on my plane from Atlanta to Memphis?
Thank God they didn't find one.

Camae   Just another day on the job.

King   Mmmhmm.

Camae   Civil rights'll kill ya fo' them Pall Malls will.

Beat. They look at each other. Then laugh really, really hard.

King   I like your sense of humor. Like mine . . . morbid.

They laugh harder and harder . . . BOOM! Crickle, CRACK. The
*thunder rolls. **King** jumps, terribly frightened.*

(*Slightly embarrassed, laughing it off.*) Wheew! Thought they
got me!

He puts his hand over his chest. He begins to breathe hard.

Camae   You all right! You all right!

King   Yes. Yes. I am.

He tries to collect himself.

Camae   Don't tell me a grown man like you 'fraid of a lil'
lightnin'?

King   No. (*Beat.*) No, that's not what I'm afraid of.

Camae   Oh. The thunder?

King   Yes, the sound. It sounds like –

Camae   Fireworks.

He contemplates this for a spell.

King   Yes. Indeed it does.

Camae   Don't be scurred of a lil' fireworks. I loves me some fireworks. Mama used to take us on down to Tom Lee Park to see the fireworks every Fourth of July.

King   Independence Day.

Camae   That right, y'all bougie black folk call it Independence Day. I can't seem to quite call it that yet.

King   You sho'll is pretty, Camae.

Camae   That 'bout the third time you done tole me that.

King   Second.

Camae   The first time you told me witcho eyes.

King   You saw me?

Camae   Hell, a blind man coulda seen't the way you was borin' holes through my clothes. Awww, you blushin'?

King (*nods his head*)   Which is really hard for a black man to do. I'm embarrassed.

Camae   Shuga, shush. You just a man. If I was you, I'd be starin' at me, too.

King   Well, I guess it's your turn to forgive me.

Camae   Forgiven and forgotten.

King   Thank you, Camae. For the . . . *square*?

Camae   I got some family from Detroit. That what they call 'em up there.

King   So you've been to Detroit? How'd you like it?

Camae   I said I got family from up there. I ain't never been.

King   Don't.

Camae   Why?

King   Negro folks done seemed to have lost their manners up there. Like to riot and carry on.

Camae   Honey, I need to move up there then. 'Cause these white folks down here 'bout to be catchin' flies now the way they be actin wit' Negroes these days. I need to catch the first Greyhound up there. Detroit niggah heaven, you axe me.

King   So are you an honorary Panther?

She growls like a panther, she's pretty good.

Camae   Walkin' will only get you so far, Preacher Kang.

King   We're not just walking: we're marching.

Camae   Whatever it is, it ain't workin'.

King   It doesn't work when you have trifling Negroes who call themselves using a peaceful protest to get a free color television.

Camae   Who done did that?

King   Just last week me and my men organized a march for –

Camae   Them garbage men?

King (*correcting*)   Yes, the *sanitation workers*. Must have been thousands upon thousands of people there. Thousands! Everybody from old men to teenage girls to little boys holding up signs that read, 'I AM A MAN'. Somehow they squeezed me to the front, we linked arms and the march began. 'I AM A MAN! I AM A MAN!' we shouted. Well, we hadn't walked but one block before we heard the sound of glass breaking. I was swept up in a tornado of arms, legs, coughing, mace. I didn't wanna leave those people, Camae. I did not wanna leave them, but . . . my men pushed me into a passing car, and . . . I looked through that back window and saw such blessed peace descend into chaos. (*Beat.*) Don't they know, you can't be marchin' down the street, bust into store windows, and then go get you a free color television? We're marching for a living wage . . . not a damn color TV! It just gives these police an excuse to shoot innocent folks. Like that boy . . . that *sixteen-year-old* boy they shot. Last week? (*Quietly to himself.*) Larry Payne. Larry Payne. Larry Payne. I'll never forget his name . . . Well, we back and we gonna do it right this time. So Larry Payne won't have to have died in vain.

He peeks out of the window, talking as if **Camae** *is not there.*

King   Where is that niggah wit' my pack?

Camae   Maybe he got stuck talkin' wit' some crazy lady in a motel room, too.

King *does not laugh.*

Camae   I'm funny. Laugh.

King   I'm worried. I don't want anything to happen to him. He happen upon something in the night don't know what I'd do without him.

Camae   That your best friend?

King   More loyal than a dog. He the one called me down to the church tonight. Got me out of bed. Just ain't been feelin' right.

Camae *gazes at him softly.* **King** *shakes himself out of it.*

King   He probably downstairs wit' my brother 'nem. Don't like to hang around me too much. I done got to bein' so moody nowadays. 'Forget about last week, Martin,' he says. Forget about it . . . (*He smiles painfully.*) After the march, the papers called me 'Chicken à la King'. Said I was a Commie coward that leaves other people to clean up my mess. 'Martin *Loser* King . . .'

Camae   Seem like times been a little rough on you.

King   Who you telling? Who are you telling . . . (*He peeks out of the window.*) This rain's just relentless. Looking like a monsoon in Memphis.

Camae (*looks at him somberly*)   Well, God ain't gone stop cryin' no time soon.

He hands her his half-smoked cigarette. Beat. She takes it. She takes a long drag between her forefinger and her thumb.

King   You smoke like a man.

Camae   *You* smoke like a fruit.

King   Aww, Camae, don't use those kinda words . . .

Camae   What, you root for the fruits?

King   Indeed I do. Alla God's children got wings.

Camae   Well . . . I agrees witcha on that one. But . . . you just ain't smokin' it right.

King   Well, how am I *supposed* to smoke it?

Camae   Like it's going out of style. Like you need it. Like you want it. That's how I smoke. Make a woman feel sexy. I bet I know why you smoke.

King   Why?

Camae   To feel sexy. 'Cause you look it.

Beat.

King   Aw, Camae. Now, you really makin' me blush. (*Pause.*) I do though, don't I?

Camae   Dr. Martin Luther Kang, Jr. Smoking. Ain't that somethin'? Wish I could take a picture of it.

King   What, you with the FBI?

Camae   Naw. Something bigger.

She hands him back the cigarette. He smokes it like a 'man'. He strikes a sexy pose and blows out a circle ring. **Camae** *pretends to snap pictures.*

There ya go. Just like that. Just like that! Pull harder. Harder. If you want to lead the people you got to smoke like the people. That way the people'll listen to ya.

Beat.

King   You don't think they listen?

Camae   Oh, they listen. They go out and march. Then they get they press 'n curls ruined by fire hoses. Folk done got tired though, Preacher Kang. (*Sighs.*) Like I say, walkin' will only get us so far –

King (*annoyed*)   Well, killin' will get you hung.

Camae   Ain't nobody said nothin' 'bout no killin'. Camae all about ass whippins. How about a march for ass whippins?

King   That's not gonna do.

Camae   Well, we need to be doin' somethin' else.

King   So what are we supposed to do?

Camae   Somethin'. Somethin' else. Hell, I got bunions and corns for days.

She takes off her shoes and sits down on the bed to rub her feet.

King   Y'all Negroes always want to complain but never have another plan of action. You sound worse than Andy or, better yet, Jesse. Everybody can shoot holes in your ideas, but they can only come up with 'somethin' else'.

Camae   *I* got a plan. But . . . *I'm* just a woman. Folk'll never listen to me.

King   So if you were me, what would you do?

Camae   Really? You wanna know what lil' old me would do?

King   Yes.

Camae   You really wanna know what I'd do?

King   Yes. I. Do.

Beat.

Camae   Can I borrow yo' jacket?

King   Sure.

Camae   And yo' shoes?

*He hands them to her. She puts them on. She stands on top of one of the beds. **King** looks on in awe. She steadies herself. Throughout her speech **King** is her congregation, egging her on with well-timed sayings like, 'Well!' 'Preach!' Or 'Make it plain!'*

Camae (*with a 'King' voice*)   Chuuch! We have gathered
here today to deal with a serious issue. It is an issue of great
paponderance – you like that? – paponderance! It is a matter of
importance more serious than my overgrown mustache: *how do
we deal with the white man?* I have told you that the white man
is our brother. And he should be treated as such. We touch our
brother with the softest of hands. We greet our brother with the
widest of smiles. We give our brother food when he is hungry. But
it is hard to do this when our brother beats his fist upon our flesh.
When he greets us with 'Nigger' and 'Go back to Africa', when he
punches us in our bellies swelling with hunger. Abel was slain by
his brother Cain and, just like the Biblical times, today the white
man is killing his Negro brethren, shackling his hands, keeping us
from rising to the stars we are booooouuuuund to occupy. We have
walked. Our feet swelling with each step. We have been drowned
by hoses. Our dreams being washed away. We have been bitten by
dogs. Our skin forever scarred by hatred at its height. Our godly
crowns have been turned into ashtrays for white men at lunch
counters all across the South. To this I say, my brethren, a new day
is coming. I'm sick and tired of being sick and tired, and today is
the day that I tell you to KILL the white man! (*Sotto voce.*) But
not with your hands. Not with your guns. But with your miiiind!
(*Back to regular voice.*) We are fighting to sit at the same counter,
but *why*, my brothers and sisters? We should build our own
counters. Our own restaurants. Our own neighborhoods. Our own
schools. The white man ain't got nothin' I want. Fuck the white
man! *Fuck* the white man! I say, FUCK 'em!

Camae *looks to* **King** *sooooo embarrassed.*

Camae   I AM SO SORRY! Preacher, Kang. Oooooo. I just
can't control my mouth.

King   Obviously, neither can I.

She steps down off the bed. And begins to pull off his jacket.

Camae   Well, you axed. That's what I would say . . . *if* . . . I
was you.

King   That's what you would have me say?

Camae   Why not?

King   'Fuck the white man'? (*Long heavy beat.*) I likes that. I think that'll be the title of my next sermon.

Camae   Oooooo! Folks ain't gone know what to do with that.

King   Amen! Fuck 'em!

Camae   I never thought I'd hear you say that!

King   Ooooo! They got me so tired, Camae. All this rippin' and runnin', rippin' and runnin' around this entire world, and for what? FOR WHAT? White folks don't seem to want to listen. Maybe you're right. Maybe the voice of violence is the only voice white folks'll listen to. (*He coughs.*) I'm tired of shoutin' and carryin' on, like you say. I'm hoarse.

He grabs **Camae**'s *flask and drinks.*

King   Sometimes I wonder where they get it from. This hatred of us. I have seen so many white people hate us, Camae. Bombin' folks' homes. Shootin' folks . . . blowin' up children.

Camae   Make you scared to bring a Negro child into this world the way they be blowin' 'em up.

King   Yes, Camae! They hate so easily, and we love too much.

Camae   Last time I heard you was preachin' 'everybody the same'. Negro folk. White folk. We all alike.

King   Well, at the most human level we *are* all the same.

Camae   What one thing we all got in common?

Beat. He searches hard to come up with an answer.

King   We scared, Camae. We all scared. Scared of each other. Scared of ourselves. They just scared. Scared of losin' somethin' that they've known their whole lives. Fear makes us human. We all need the same basic things. A hug. A smile. A –

Camae   Smoke?

King (*frustrated*)   Which I could use one more of. Where is that niggah wit' my pack?

Camae *goes to the window, but can't see past the rain.*

King   He always out there runnin' his mouth. Worse than me sometimes. You see him?

Camae   Naw.

King   He'll be back. He know I don't like to be alone too long . . .

Beat. He looks back towards **Camae**.

King   I just wish you had another one. To share, of course.

Camae *pulls another pack of Pall Malls from her maid's uniform.* **King** *stands confused.*

King   I thought you gave me your last one?

Camae   I did. But I'm a magician. I got more where that came from.

King   More tricks up your sleeve?

Camae   Well, as you can tell . . . I ain't yo' ordinary ole maid.

He looks her up and down.

King   Certainly. Certainly! Not too many maids spouting off well-formed diatribes like that.

Camae   What, you thank us po' folk can't talk? You thank we dumb?

King   Naw, naw, that's not what I said, now –

Camae   You thank you always gotta talk for us?

King   No, that's not what I said –

Camae   Then what you sayin'?

King   I'm sayin' . . . that most maids don't sound like professors.

Camae   Well, let me school you, you bougie Negro. I don't

need no PhD to give you some knowledge, understand. Divinity
school? *Huh!* You don't know who you *messin' wit'*!

King   Well, Camae, I just . . . I just like ya style. Didn't mean
to offend ya. Just wanted to compliment ya. You sang it real pretty.

She calms down.

Camae   Well . . . tell me . . . how are my 'oratorical skills' – see
ye'en thank I knew them words – How are my *oratorical skills*
compared to –

King   Mine?

Camae   Sho.

Beat.

King   I'm better.

Camae   Awww, really, now?

King   You made it sound real pretty, now, but really . . . *I'm*
better. Nobody can make it pretty like me. I've been doing this for
years, darlin'. Gonna be doin' it till the day I die.

Camae   But was it good?

King   For a woman, yes.

Camae   And if I was a man?

King   Then you'd be Malcolm X.

Camae   So, you callin' Malcolm X a sissy?

King   No, that's not what I said, Miss Camae.

Camae   You callin' Malcolm X a sissy!

King   No, I'm not, Camae.

Camae   I'ma tell it on you!

*She runs and opens up the door and screams at the top of her
lungs into the pouring night sky.*

MALCOLM, MARTIN THANK YOU A SISSY!!!

King   CAMAE! Come from out that door! / You gone get STRUCK!

Camae   You hear that, Malcolm! He callin' you A SISSY!!

The thunder rolls and **Camae** *laughs at the sky threatening to crackle again.*

(*To Malcolm in the sky.*) I'd strike him down for that, too, if I was you.

King *grabs her by the waist and slams the door.*

King   Didn't your mama teach you how to be still when it's thundering and lightning?

Camae   Didn't I tell you I was hard-headed and ain't mind her one bit?

King   Well, God don't like to be laughed at.

Camae   Why? I laugh at God all the time. God funny as Hell. God a fuuuunnny-ass muthafucka.

Beat.

King   I don't like the way you talk about God. You might need to leave you blasphemin' God like that.

Beat.

Camae   I was just tryin' to make you laugh. Bring a little laughter to your life. I like makin' folks laugh, Preacher Kang. God knows you need it –

King   I don't mind laughin'. I like a good joke. Got to. Nowadays. I just don't like how you talk about God.

Camae   I'm sorry. God don't mind it. God ain't like siddity folk. God even like dirty jokes.

King   How you know what God like?

Camae   'Cause I do. I know God liked Malcolm X. And you woulda liked him, too. He didn't drank. Smoke. Cuss. Or . . . Cheat. On. His Wife.

Beat.

King (*wryly*)   And how are you privy to this information?

She stares him down.

Camae   Like, I said befo', Negro talk strike faster than lightnin'. (*Pause.*) Did you ever meet him?

King   Once. But we never got a chance to really –

Camae   Talk?

King   Before he got –

Camae   Killed? (*Pause.*) That's a shame.

King   He was only thirty-nine. (*To himself.*) I'm thirty-nine . . .

Pause.

Camae   He in heaven.

King   Is that right?

Camae   You'll see him there . . . One day.

King   Camae, you talk a lot of nonsense sometimes.

Camae   Nonsense comin' out of a pretty woman's mouth ain't nonsense at all. It's poetry.

King   No, I think that's – what would yo' kinda folk say – *bullshit*?

Camae   Oooooo, I likes it when ya feathers get ruffled. You get all blunt. It look cute on you. But you will. In heaven.

King   So you think he in heaven right now?

Camae   Why wouldn't he be?

King   I don't know, now. He talked a lot of –

Camae   Truth?

King   A lot of violence. He had a weakness for violent words. Speak by the sword, die by the sword –

Camae   Speak by love, die by hate. (*Pause.*) We all have
weaknesses, Preacher Kang. I'm sho' you got yo' own. Just ain't
never let nobody . . . know. (*Beat.*) For what it worth, I know God
like *you*. The real *you*.

King   Do He really?

Camae   *She* likes you.

King   *She?*

Camae   She told me She like you. That if you was in heaven,
you'd be her husband.

King (*smiles a big toothy grin*)   Oh, Camae! Is that what God
said?

Camae   Yeap.

King   So God in love with me?

Camae   She ain't 'in love', She 'in like'! In like with her some
Dr. Kang.

King   I think God ain't told you nothin'. I think it's you who
want me for yo' husband.

Camae   Mmmm. Me and God ain't got the same taste. I don't
like no man wit' no smelly feet.

King   They do stink, don't they? Don't tell nobody.

Camae   Honey, yo' shoes off. I thank the whole world know by
now. Who woulda thunk Dr. Kang got stanky feet. Oooo! And you
got holes in yo' socks, too?

King *laughs at her. At himself.*

King   You make it easy.

Camae   Make what easy?

King   To make a man forget about it all. About . . . all . . . this . . .

Camae   That what I'm here for.

King   What else you here for?

He has begun to take off his tie. He struggles a bit. He's gotten stuck.

Camae What, you tryin' to lynch yoself? Here let me help ya.

They stand face to face. Close. **Camae** *slowly untangles him from it. He stares into her face. Transfixed. He reaches up to touch her face. She smiles.*

King Thank you.

Camae You welcome.

BOOM! BOOM! Crickle! CRACK! **King** *stumbles back in a daze. Faint. He begins to hold his chest.*

Camae You awright?

King I can't breathe.

Camae Well, I've been known to have that effect on mens.

King No, I mean. I can't. I can't / can't, can't can't breathe.

Camae Oh, my God. Oh, God! / Did I do something wrong?

King I can't can't can't / breathe. I can't breathe.

Camae Oh, my God! I did / something wrong! I did something!

King Can't can't / can't can't can't can't breathe . . .

Camae Just look into my eyes./ Just look right there.

King I can't. I can't. I can't.

Camae Michael?

King Can't can't / can't –

Camae Michael! Michael! MICHAEL!! Michael, just breathe!

King (*sotto voce*) – can't can't / can't can't . . .

Camae I'ma get you through this. I'ma get you through this night.

Just as soon as it starts, the thunder in **King***'s heart stops, and he*

sits stunned, staring at **Camae***. Silence. They breathe together . . .
in . . . out . . . in . . . out . . . in . . . out . . . in . . .*

King   You called me Michael.

Camae (*knowing she did*)   I did?

King   Yes. You. Did. You called me Michael.

Camae   You – you – scared me –

King   How would you know that?

Camae   Know what?

King   To call me that?

Camae   Call you what?

King   YOU KNOW WHAT THE HELL I'M TALKING
ABOUT.

Camae   Calm, down Mich – I mean, Preacher Kang. I didn't
mean to call you out yo' name –

King   But that *is* my name. My childhood name. How do you
know my real name? My Christian name?

He slowly backs away from her.

(*Softly.*) Oh. So, you one of them, huh?

Camae   I'm so sorry. I never wanted to do this. This is so hard
for me to do –

King (*shaking his head*)   An *incognegro*. A spy.

Camae   I was sent to –

King   WHAT? Tempt me?

Camae   Hell, you was the one tempting me, getting me all off
my job!

King   I don't wanna hear it. Get out.

Camae   No.

King   I said get out. You spook.

Camae   I was only doing my job –

King   I said GET OUT! Coming in here tempting me!

Enraged, **King** *overturns the furniture, searching for bugs he may have glossed over.*

Camae   Preacher Kang!

King (*yelling to no one in particular*)   What, y'all think you can trap me! Record me with a woman! Well, you're not going to catch me!

Camae   Preacher Kang, stop / acting so paranoid!

King   Sending tapes to my wife. Tryin' to break up my family. Tryin' to break my spirit!

Camae   Preacher Kang, calm down!

King   You think you can break me! (*Screaming to no one in particular.*) Well, *you* can't break me! You WILL NEVER BREAK ME AGAIN!

King *grabs* **Camae** *by her arm and aggressively pulls her towards the door.*

Camae   You're hurting me! Preacher / Kang, you're hurting me!!

King   How much they pay you, you *spook*? How much?

Camae   Let go, you're hurting me!!!

King   Where the hell is Ralph? Ralph! I got a spook!

Camae   You wrong! You wrong!

King   Where in the *hell* is Ralph?

HEY!

He opens the door. A wall of snow covers the doorway.

HEEEeeeey . . .

A huge gust of wind blows in snow that piles at his feet. He lets go of **Camae**'s *arm. He stands in awe. Looking at the snow.*

King   It's snowing . . . in April.

Camae   It snow sometimes in spring. Here. In Memphis.

He looks back at her. He looks back at the snow at his feet. He looks back at her again. Beat. He closes the door. Then opens it again. He blinks.

King   It's still there. The snow. It's still there.

Camae   As it should be.

He closes the door again.

King   No, no, no, I'm just tired. I'm tired. I'm seeing things that ain't there.

Camae   Oh, it's there.

King   No, it's not. Tell me it's not.

He pulls the curtains back from the windows. They, too, are filled to the brim with snow.

Camae   See, it's there.

King   No. No. No. You've drugged me. Slipped something in my coffee. Some hippie pills in my coffee! Got me seeing things that ain't there.

Camae   I just put some whiskey up in there to relax you –

King   You put some hippie pills in my coffee! Made me see. Snow. Snow? Snow . . .

He opens the door again and sees the snow is still there. His heart threatens to jump out of his chest.

I can't can't can't go anywhere. I can't get out. I can't get *out*!

Camae   Relax! *Calm down!*

He rushes to the phone. Picks it up.

King   Help! HELP! No dial tone.

Camae   Michael!

King   Quit calling me that! QUIT CALLING ME THAT!!

Camae *lunges toward him. He jumps over the bed.*

Camae   We need to calm you down! You gone give yoself a heart attack. You might be thirty-nine but you got the heart of a sixty-year-old man.

King   I can't can't can't go. I can't can't.

He backs himself against the wall.

Camae   Michael! / Shhhhh!!

King   How do you know so much about me! Who in the Hell are you? WHO IN THE HELL ARE YOU?

Camae *blows on the end of a cigarette. It lights up.* **King** *stands stunned. Looong aaaass beat.*

King   Wow.

Camae   I know. Angel breath is some hot breath.

King   You're. An. Angel?

Camae   In the flesh.

King   So, where are your wings?

She points to her breasts.

Camae   These'll get me anywhere I need to go.

King   Wow. An angel?

Camae   Yes. I'm here to take you to the other side.

King   The other side. So I'm not dead?

Camae   No. Not yet.

Beat.

King   Wheew! 'Cause I was about to get mad if heaven looked like this.

They look around the room that's been torn apart in their tussle.

(*Suddenly very serious.*) I'm not going to hell, am I?

Camae   Naw. Naw. Naw! Heaven is where we headed.

King (*with wide eyes*)   Good. Good. Good. Do all angels look as good as you?

Camae   Yes.

King   Heaven must be mighty nice then. I wonder what the women in hell look like?

Camae   Honey, they finer. Why you thank they in hell?

King   Camae, you're really an angel?

He looks at her incredulous. She nods her head.

Camae   Sorry, I called you Michael. Not too many folk prolly know that 'bout you. God said that yo' Christian name kinda calms you. Ralph call you that, too. Calms you down quick fast. It a nice name. It ain't better than Camae, though.

King   I changed it / when my daddy did.

Camae   When yo' daddy did. When you was just five. I done read yo' file. But I don't know why y'all wanna be named after some Martin Luther though. I met him in the cafeteria today and he was kinda weird. Very.

He slowly circles **Camae**.

King   You're really an angel?

Camae   What else I got to do for you to believe me? Cry flowers?

King   But but – but why God send *you*?

Pause.

Camae   What you mean by that?

King Why He –

Camae *She!*

King *She* send you? You're not what I was expecting.

Camae Shiiiit, you wun't what *I* was expecting, *Preacher* Kang!

King Well, I'm not perfect.

Camae That you ain't!

King Hey, hey, don't judge me, you cussin', fussin' drankin' angel!

Camae Well, God know what you like, henh!

King Hey, hey that ain't fair now!

Camae The truth ain't gotsta to be fair. It's the truth.

King But *why* you?

Camae Believe you me I ain't want this job. First day? Bring over you? The Kang? I ain't wanna do it. But God been gettin' these prayers from a littl'un named Bunny.

A voice flutters out of **Camae***'s mouth like a butterfly. It softly lands inside the room.*

'Please, God, don't let my daddy die alone.' When I heard it . . . Well, it just 'bout broke my heart. I just had to come . . .

Camae *actually does start to cry, and flowers bloom at her feet.*

Beat.

King You know her nickname . . . Bernice, my sweet Bernice. My baby girl spoke to you?

Camae Her prayers are powerful. I can tell she's yourn. She gots a way with words. A gift. Soundin' like she gone be a preacher one day. I don't like chiren too much, but she . . . she somethin'.

King My Bunny, my baby girl. Even she knows . . .

Camae   Yes. I gotta take you to the other side. (*Pause.*) Look, I know you afraid, Preacher Kang –

King   How you know I'm afraid?

Camae   Because . . . You should be.

She points to the door of the motel. Beneath the door burns bright red. The door begins to bulge and wave as fingers begin to push and poke through the door. **King** *slowly walks towards the door, drawn to the danger, drawn to the bullet . . .*

King (*with total calm*)   You talk about fear, Camae, well . . . I have felt fear. Felt it in my guts. Felt it in my toes. Felt it even when I stood in front of my own congregation in my own church. There beneath that old rugged cross, I quaked and shook with fear. My insides churned and I fought hard to keep them from leaping out of my mouth. You see, a Negro man is not safe in a pulpit. Not even in a pulpit of his own making. Sunday mornings have been the mornings when I am most afraid. 'Cause in this country a pulpit is a pedestal and we all know that, in America, the tall tree is felled first. Tall trees have more wood to burn, Camae. We are the sacrifice.

Camae   You been knowin' I was comin', haven't you?

King   Yes. Oh, yes. I have dreamed of you. Rather had nightmares. In my darkest hours, I've even prayed for you with eyes wide open. Been so many death threats that some nights I have asked God, 'Please just get it over with.' Even tonight at the church . . .

He softly cups her face in his hand.

Who knew death would be so beautiful? Almost make a man wanna die.

Camae   You not afraid of me?

King   Fear has become my companion, my lover. I know the touch of fear, even more than I know the touch of my own wife. Fear, Camae, is my best friend. She is the reason I get up in the morning. 'Cause I know if I'm still afraid, then I am still alive.

Camae   Tomorrow. When it time, you gone have to take my hand.

King   Tomorrow? But I'm not ready to die. I still got so much work to do.

Camae   But God say it time.

King   No, it's not my time. I ain't ready. I still have so much work to do.

He points to the papers back at his desk and he goes to sit down. He writes:

King (*to* **Camae**)   'Why America is going to hell – '

Camae   Preacher Kang, now you / gone have to put that down.

King (*'King voice' back on*)   A country that sends its boys to bathe little-bitty brown babies in the blood of our greed is headed for a crossroads of conscience –

Camae   You hear what I said, you ain't gone be able to finish that, nanh.

King – And the consequence? Our young are flown back home in star-strangled coffins. Unwashable our hands as we stand at Heaven's gates, wondering why our God will not let us in. And why won't He?

Camae   She!!

King   She let us in? Cause America is going to Hell! Cast down like Lucifer in the pit to burn, baby burn!

Camae (*under her breath*)   And I thought I was the radical.

King   A tsunami of rage is rolling across the bottom of our seas and America, my sweet America, is surrounded by rising water, waiting to drown. Pharaohs will be overthrown when that great wave of change casts them into the roiling waters! But the children of the Nile will rise, they will RISE, my brethren!! Can I get an Amen? I SAID can I get an Amen?

Camae   AMEN!!

King (*panting, spent from his inspiration*)   See, that'll make a good sermon, won't it?

Camae   Hell, I'd sit in a pew for a few for that one.

King   So you agree with me? Well, I gots to finish my sermon and I need to be alone to finish my sermon so . . . you gone have to fly on away.

He continues scribbling with his pen, fast and furiously.

Camae   Preacher Kang –

King   Exactly one year ago, I stood in that pulpit at Riverside Church and shouted that this war would be our own violent undoing, freedom's suicide . . . Well, I'll tell you, there weren't too many Amens that Sunday. But who is a man who does not speak his heart's conscience? He is not a man, but I *am* a man. If only they could see that love is the most radical weapon there is. But they won't listen. Instead, they have called me every name in the book but a child of God. Even my own men – 'You splitting the movement, Martin, you splittin' the movement! You can't focus on war, and poverty, *and* Negroes!'

Camae   Well, ain't you just a civil rights leader? You can't be talkin' bout war, then this, then that.

King   And why the hell not?

Camae   Who you thank you is, the President? You can't call all the shots, all the time –

King (*under his breath*)   Just for a little bit more time, just a little bit more . . .

Still writing.

America, America –

Camae   Preacher Kang, –

King   – *my country tis of thee* –

Camae   You makin' my job harder –

King – *my country who doles out constant misery* –

Camae – harder than it already is –

King – *war abroad, then war in* your *streets, Arrogant America.*

Camae – this HARD on me.

King (*bolting from his desk*) Hard on *you*? What about it bein' hard on me? On my family? On Corrie? On the movement? HAS GOD THOUGHT ABOUT THAT?!

Camae God ain't the one you need to be mad at while you up there yellin'! God ain't the one you need to be blamin' –

King Then who needs to be blamed?

Camae It ain't *who* needs to be blamed, Preacher Kang. It's *what*. It ain't a *who*, it's a *what*, Preacher Kang. Evil is not under God's jurisdiction. But good, *good* is.

King Well, can't you stop it? Catch whatever's coming?

Camae That ain't my job. God said I gotta get you ready to come on home.

King But we still got work to do. I got more sermons in me, more goals, more . . . plans!

He gets down on bended knee.

Camae, I wanna do another March on Washington. Bigger. Better. Bolder.

Camae Another *dream* of yours?

King But I wanna make *this* one a reality! The plan. It's all in the works. It's called the Poor People's Campaign!

Camae Poor People's Campaign? What that is? It bet' not be no 'nother march. You / and yo' marches.

King Listen to me.

Camae You and yo / marches!

King Please, Camae! Listen!

She sits down on the bed and starts eating popcorn out of her maid's uniform.

Camae   I'm listening. Gone.

King   We've been organizing this campaign all year. All year. Imagine, Camae. On the Washington Mall, not thousands, but millions –

Camae   Millions of Negroes on the Washington Mall? / Shiiiiiit.

King   No, no, not just Negroes. White folk, Chinese folk, Mexican folk, Indian folk, all banding together to shame this country. All kinds of poor folks pulling their mule wagons across the Washington Mall. A rainbow of people chanting, 'Stop the war on Vietnam! Start the war on poverty!'

Camae   Unh, unh! How 'bout 'Make love! Not poverty!'?

King   Hey, I like that one, too! They can call me Commie King all they like, I don't care. I refuse to allow poor people to be cast aside along this Jericho Road! That's why we had to come here. Not to walk, but to march. Peacefully. Memphis is just a dress rehearsal for the big one. *Memphis* is just the beginning.

Camae   Yo' men'll carry it on.

King   But I'm the leader of this movement. The head of the body.

Camae   Well, the body will just have to grow another head 'cause Memphis is the end of the road for you.

King   End of the road? But . . . but . . . can't you . . . can't you ask God?

Camae   Honey, I can't do you no kinda special / favors!

King   Just till next month? Till I see this plan on through? Just till April 29th.

Camae   And what if She let you? You just gone keep on saying one more day, one more month, one more this, one more that!

King   No, I won't.

Camae   Yes, you will! I know you, Preacher Kang.

King   But I have so much work to do –

Camae   But what about yo' mens? Can't they see it through?

King   They don't dream the same dreams I do, Camae. They think I'm crazy to dream this big, and maybe I am a little crazy, but how can we fight the war in Vietnam but not the wars against Negroes in our streets? How can we try to put a man on the moon but not feed starving children in Mississippi? There's just so much I gotta do. So much I haven't yet accomplished. So much . . . I GOTTA FINISH WHAT I STARTED!!

Camae   It ain't all about you! *You! You!* Gosh, you men are so selfish. They always thank it's 'bout them. Them! *Them!* Hah! Well, let me tell you something, Preacher Kang. Let me tell you! Like most men, you ain't gone be able to finish what you started.

King   My house has been bombed! I have been pelted wit' rocks. My arm twisted behind my back. My face shoved into a ground of gravel. I have been kicked at. Spit at. Pummelled. Abused. Looked at with the deepest scorn. I have been stabbed in my chest. And I walked away. Alive! Alive! If I woulda sneezed I woulda died.

Camae (*under her breath*)   Well, I'm glad you ain't have no cold that day.

King (*ignoring her*)   Look at the life I've lived. You tell me I ain't got favor wit' God! After all that? Tell me I ain't jumped over every hurdle of this race!

Camae   Well, sometimes you done cleared the hurdles and sometimes . . . you ain't. Remember Albany? You done brought us far. But you a man. You just a man, baby. You're not God, though some folk'll say you got mighty close. You know . . . sometimes, you've failed.

Beat. The wind sinks out of his sails.

King   Like when that boy . . . that boy got shot. Larry Payne.

Camae   Well, *that* wun't yo' fault. Police killed that boy. Not you.

Beat. **Camae** *stands silent.*

King   . . . So this motel room will become my tomb? But I have survived so much . . .

Camae   Honey, I know all about your trials and tribulations. I done read yo' blessings file. It bigger than yo' FBI file and that bigga than the Bible. I know it might be hard for you to leave this life . . . yo' family . . . and all yo' plans. But you gone have to pass off that baton, little man. You in a relay race, albeit the fastest runner we done ever seen't. But you 'bout to burn out, superstar. You gone need to pass off that baton . . .

Beat.

King   I know I have dropped this baton so many times over this race. But I promise, I ain't gonna do it again. Tell Her.

Camae   *Tell* Her?

King   Yes, tell Her I promise, I won't ever drop this baton again. Tell Her, She needs to let me stay. Ask Her. For me.

Camae (*hissing*)   You ain't supposed to question God. That's the rule. You know that!

King   There ain't no rules for an angel like you!

Camae   Shhiiiit! God gots rules! I had to read the whole Bible today –

King   Please. Camae.

Camae   Dr. KANG!

King   PLEASE!!

Pause.

Camae   Well . . . whatchoo gone give *me*?

King (*smiles seductively*)   A kiss from the Kang.

Camae   I don't want no kiss from you, 'cause you ain't brushed yo' teeth.

King   Please, Camae . . .

He goes down on bended knee. He plucks one of the flowers from the carpet and hands it to her in submission. Beat.

Camae (*disgusted*)   Ughhh.

She snatches it from him. She walks over to the rotary phone on the night stand beside the bed. She dials a really long phone number.

You lucky I 'member this. This just my first day.

She waits and waits . . . and waits. Finally, someone on the other end picks up. **King** *sits beside* **Camae** *and tries to listen in on the conversation.*

Camae   Hey, St Augustine. What up? Yeah . . . Can I speak to God? (*Beat.*) What She doin'? (*Pause.*) Ohhhh . . . (*To* **King**.) There are some forest fires. She had to go make some rain and – (*To St Augustine.*) Unh, hunh. When She gone be back? Well . . . Can you call her cell phone? 'Cause this man is really gettin' on my nerves. I'm tryin' to get him on the program. Yeah, I KNOW!! That's what I tried to tell him. You know . . . Martyrs. (*Pause.*) Sho' can. (*To* **King**.) He tryin' to get her on the cell.

King   The cell?

Camae   It's like . . . a phone that ain't got no cord.

King   A phone wit' no cord?

Camae   Sorta like when you talkin' to God. Don't need no real cord, She just sorta . . . answers –

Beat. She perks up. Someone has come to the phone.

Camae   Hello there, God. It's me. Camae. Mmmhmmm. How it goin'? (*She looks at* **King**.) It goin' pretty good. Yep. Yeah, I'm halfway through my shift. Taking a break . . . but . . . uhm . . . Well, there's a bit of problem. (*She pulls the phone away from her ear.*) He say he ain't ready. (*God yells at her ass again.*) That what I told him. I know . . . I know . . . I KNOW.

King   Let me talk to Her.

Camae   No –

King   I wanna talk to yo' supervisor!

Camae *puts her hand over the phone.*

Camae   Shhh! I'm tryin' to butter Her up first.

King   Butter Her up? Let me talk to Her!!

He tries to snatch the phone from **Camae**.

Camae   Hold on a got gum minute, Preacher Kang! (*Pause.*) Yes. But he stubborn! (*She looks at him.*) And quite convincing. He sho'll do got a way wit' words. I know you told me. You wanna talk to him? Well, good. 'Cause he wanna talk to You.

She hands the phone over to him. **King** *snatches it. Clears his throat. Puts the phone to his ear. Beat.*

King   Uhm. God? It's uhmm . . . (*Putting on his 'King voice'.*) Dr. Martin Luther King, J – oh, yes. Michael, to you . . . Yes Ma'am . . . yes Ma'am . . . yes . . . Ma'am. (*He pulls the phone from his ear and whispers.*) Is She –

Camae   Black? Mmhm. And PROUD . . .

King *puts the phone back to his ear.*

King   God, Ma'am, You don't sound like I thought You'd sound. No, no, no. Pardon me, if that offends. I like how You sound. Kinda like my grandmama. Well . . . it is a compliment. I loved her dearly . . . I love You more, though. Camae told me that you might be busy tonight. Oh, You have time for me? For one of Your favorites?

He smiles at **Camae**, *who rolls her eyes.*

King   God, are You all right? You sound hoarse. Oh, You tired? Well, it must be tiring to be everywhere all at the same time (*He laughs nervously.*) Well, God . . . I don't mean to trouble You, Ma'am, but I wanted to ask You something . . . You see I have always listened to You, honored Your word, lived by Your word – (*He lowers his voice.*) for the most part – (*Raises it back to normal.*) God, please don't strike me down for askin' this, but . . . I want to live. I have plans. Lots of plans in my head and in my heart and my people need me. They need me. And I need to see them to the Promised Land. (*Beat.*) I know that's not what I said earlier tonight, I know, but . . . I wasn't lying exactly. (*He looks at* **Camae**.) I just didn't know she was comin' so, so . . . soon. I meant every word I said tonight when I spoke to those people. Dead honest! No pun intended . . . God, I just . . . I wanna see my people there, the tide is turning . . . war is becoming the order of the day and I must, I must convince them to be vigilant . . . We've come too far to turn back now . . . God, listen to me . . . Who else is betta fit for this job? I mean, who will take my place? (*He hears Her answer.*) JESSE?! (*Pause.*) I – I – I just thought Ralph would make a better – No, no, no, no, I have not turned vain. On the contrary. I'm but a servant for You, God, Ma'am. Yes, I've been a servant for You all my life. At one point in time, I might nota been up for the challenge but I knew this was all par for the course and I did Your will. I honored YOUR WILL, God, Ma'am. Let me not die a man who doesn't get to hug his children one last time. Let me not die a man who never gets to make love to his wife one last time. Let me not be a man who dies afraid and alone. (*Long pause.*) Then why'd You pick me, huh? Hmm, no disrespect, but if You didn't know what I could do, what my (*hissing*) *talents* were then . . . You got some nerve. Dragging me here to this moldy motel room in Memphis. To die. HUH! Of all places! Well, I *am* angry. There have been many a' nights when I have held my tongue when it came to You. But not tonight, NOT TONIGHT. I have continuously put my life on the line, gave it all up. Gave it all up for You and Your word. You told me, that'd I'd be safe. Safe in Your arms. You protected me all this time, all this time! Glued a pair of wings to my back, but now that've I've flown too close to the sun I'm falling into the ocean of death. God how dare You take me now? NOW! I beg of You. I plead – God? Ma'am? God?

Long heavy silence.

Camae (*whispers from the corner*)   What She say?

King   I think . . . I think she hung up on me.

Camae   Hmm. Coulda been a dropped call.

Pause.

King   A dropped call? How does one 'drop' a call? This angel talk you speak . . .

Camae   You act like I'm speakin' in tongues.

King   Well, you speak of things I know nothing about.

Camae   Yes. I speak of the future.

King   The future?

Camae (*aggressively*)   Ooooo!! YOU DONE GOT ME IN TROUBLE!! God gone tan my hide from brown to barbecue.

King   How did I get *you* in trouble?

Camae   Look, I can't just call Her for you! You gone make me lose my wings.

She rubs her breasts.

King   Good, you need to lose them! Maybe you'll stop luring men to their deaths! (*Pause.*) I can't believe She hung up on me.

Camae   I woulda hung up on you, too. Yellin' like that.

King   God hung up on me. She forsook her servant.

Camae   She ain't forsake you neither. She just ain't wanna hear yo' shit. She got the right. She is God, ya know?

King   And I am Dr. King, *ya know*?

Beat.

Camae   Don't mark me, man . . .

King   *Ya know? Ya know?*

Camae   I do *not* sound like that.

King   Least you don't say, ya dig? *Ya dig? Ya dig?* Like a Black

Panther Party angel! That's how you would sound if you said it, too. *Ya dig?*

Camae   Ohhh.

She picks up a pillow lying on the bed and pelts him with it.

King   Camae! God gonna get you. Beatin' up one of Her favorites like this!

Camae   Can't believe she done sent me to come get you witcho crazy ass.

She pelts him with a pillow again and again. **King** *picks up a pillow to protect himself. She misses him this time. Laughs heartily.*

Camae   You thank you so funny, Preacher Man.

King   That's right! Hit me! Hit me if you think you bad!

He is quick and surprisingly good at pillow-fighting. He clobbers her over the head with the pillow.

Camae   OW!

King   That's what you get for battling the Kang of pillow-fightin'!

He pummels her again with the pillow. She flies across the bed.

Camae   You can't hit angels with pillows!

King   Where is that rule?

Camae   In the Bible!

King   Unh, unh! Where?

Camae   Ezekiel, fool!

She clobbers him one good time. He falls on to the bed. Her pillow bursts and feathers flutter out. Spilling across the room. He hits her back, and his pillow bursts. More feathers fly across the room. They laugh. They laugh as feathers are falling. Falling everywhere like the rain was before and the snow was before. There is a feather blizzard inside Room 306 at the Lorraine Motel. And **King** *and his death angel roll in the feather storm of their own making. Their pillows, now devoid of fluff, are tossed to the wayside and then* **King** *takes* **Camae** *and starts tickling her.*

Camae   Stop it!

King   I bet you're ticklish.

Camae   Don't tickle me!

King   Why?

Camae   'Cause I'ma pee on you!

King   Angels don't pee.

Camae   Try me. That's in the Bible, too.

King   No, it's not!

Camae   Watch out, my piss gone burn you! Tsssss!

King   I don't believe you.

Camae   You betta!

He tickles her.

I'm peein'! STOP! I'm peein'!

He finally somehow pins **Camae** *on to her back. He is on top of her. They stop. Gazing into each other's eyes. Out of breath. A bit sweaty.*

King   I never thought death would be so beautiful.

Camae   Sometimes. Tonight's a good night. I remembered my rouge.

Beat.

King   Camae?

Camae   Yes, Preacher Kang.

King   Hold me.

Beat. **King***'s eyes well with tears and this strong, grown man dissolves into the child no one ever saw. He slides down on top of her. Crying. Crying his heart out. Sobbing. And* **Camae** *holds him. And rubs his back as if he were a child.*

Camae (*softly*)   There . . . there . . . let it all out. Give it all to me. I will take it all . . . there . . . there . . . give it all to me.

King (*hiccupping like children do*)   I've been prayin' that it would stop.

Camae   There . . . there . . . / Shhhh.

King   That it would all go away. I never wanted to do this. I just wanted to be a minister in my small church.

Camae   But when your maker calls you, you must heed the call.

King   I just wanted to be a minister. That was enough. That was enough . . .

Camae   But God had bigger plans for you.

King   Why me?

Camae   Why not you?

King   'Cause I'm . . . just a man. I know now, I know. And it's time for me to come on home. Help me. Help me get my things together.

He rises and heads to his suitcase. He begins to pack it.

Camae   You won't be needing that. Won't be needing that at all. Heaven got all you need.

King *looks around the room.*

King   Well . . . I need to leave my men some instructions. Notes.

Camae   They can do it on they own.

King   But I need to tell them what to do when I'm . . . gone.

Camae   They'll know what to do. You've taught them well.

Soft pause.

King   Well . . . well . . . my wife . . . I need to call my wife . . .

He runs to the phone and dials. He sings into it again.

Corrie pick up. Corrie pick up. Corrie, Corrie Corrie pick up.

She doesn't pick up. Silence. He finally hangs up the phone. Long heavy beat.

I always bought her flowers when I went away. Always with the mind that they would last long enough till I made it home. Sometimes they would. Most times they didn't. I could never make amends, so I bought her flowers that would stand in for those passin' pockets of time just as I existed for her. I picked a beautiful flower called 'absence'. And it bloomed like dandelions, a weed she could never rid her garden of. Last week, when I was home, I walked past this shop, and I saw the most perfect flowers. Radiant red carnations. I went into the store, and, you know what I found out, Camae? They weren't real. My eyes had fooled me. But I bought those flowers, and they arrived yesterday morning just before I left to board the plane to Memphis. She came to me, with a twinkle in her eyes and said, 'Why, Martin. You never give me these old artificial things . . . ' I smiled. 'Today is different. Today . . . '

Camae   You knew she'd need a flower that could last forever.

King   If only I could tell them how sorry I am. If only I could have been there with them. I missed birthdays. I missed holidays. I –

Camae   You did what you had to do. We needed you. The world needed you.

King   Many a' times I've wanted to quit. To give up the ghost.

Camae   But you didn't. You prevailed.

King   I don't know for what! I've sacrificed my marriage, my family. My health. For what?

Camae   Powerful the man that get more done dead than alive.

King   I don't want to be a martyr.

Camae   But the suit fits you well.

King   I am a man. I am just a man.

Camae   Tomorrow, you'll be a man made martyr. No, better yet!
A saint!

King   Don't call me that. I'm a sinner, not a saint. I'm not
deservin' of the title.

Camae   You think I am?

King   You must. God must a' been impressed with how you've
lived your life –

Camae   (*quietly*)   No . . . She wun't.

She turns away.

King   But I thought angels were perfect.

Camae   You perfect?

King   No.

Camae   Then why should I be? Honey, I've robbed. I've lied.
I've cheated. I've failed. I've cursed. But what I'm ashamed of
most is, I've hated. Hated myself. Sacrificed my flesh so that
others might feel whole again. I thought it was my duty. All that
I had to offer this world. What else was a poor black woman, the
mule of the world, here for? Last night, in the back of a alley I
breathed my last breath. A man clasped his hands like a necklace
'round my throat. I stared into his big blue eyes, as my breath
got ragged and raw, and I saw the hell this old world had put him
through. The time he saw his father hang a man. The time he saw
his mother raped. I felt so sorry for him. I saw what the world had
done to him, and I still couldn't forgive. I hated him for stealing
my breath. When I passed on to the other side, God – ooooo, She
is more gorgeous than me. She the color of midnight and Her eyes
are brighter than the stars. Her hair . . . well . . . just you wait till
you see her hair – God stood there before me. With this look on
her face. I just knowed She was just soooo disappointed in me. I
was just a' cryin', weepin' at her feet. Beggin' her not to throw me

down. All that sinnin'. All that grime on my soul. All that hatred in my heart. But then I looked up and saw that She was smilin' down at me. She opened her mouth, and silence came out. But I heard her loud and clear. 'I got a special task for you and if you complete it, all your sins will be washed away.'

I opened my file. And I saw my task was you. What could little old me, give to big old you? I thought you was gone be perfect. Well, you ain't, but then you are. You have the biggest heart I done ever knownt. You have the strength to love those who could never love you back. If I had just a small fraction of the love you have for this world, then maybe, just maybe I could become half the angel you are.

Long heavy beat.

King   Will I die at the hands of a white man, too?

Beat.

Camae   Yes. Speak by love. Die by hate.

King   Where will it be?

Camae   On the balcony just right there.

They look to the door of the room.

King   How?

Camae   Surrounded by those who love you.

King   Will you be there to clean up the mess?

Camae   It would be an honor, Preacher Kang.

King   Will there be others after me? To carry on the baton?

Camae   Many, many will carry it on, but there'll never be another you. You are a once-in-a-lifetime affair.

King   Is the future as beautiful as you?

Camae   Yes . . . and it's as ugly as me, too.

King   I wanna see it.

Camae   I don't know if you could handle it. It might break your heart.

King   My heart already weary, Camae. I wanna see it before I die.

Camae   But I thought you done already seen the Promised Land?

King   In my dreams, but I wanna see it with my eyes. My own eyes. If I see – *really* see it, I will die a happy man tomorrow. I will go willingly into your arms, Camae. If you just let me see these dreams I'll never ever see.

Beat.

A trembling **King** *reaches out to* **Camae***. She doesn't take his hand.*

Camae   I'll let you see, but when you're called back you'll have to come. I'ma have to take you on home tomorrow.

King   What time shall I meet you?

Camae   6:01 p.m.

King   Is it gonna hurt?

Camae   You won't feel the hurt. The world will.

King (*teary eyed*) You promise?

Camae   I promise. You ready? **King** *nods, gulping back tears.*

Camae   Let's take you to the mountaintop.

She walks up to him and kisses him. He becomes woozy in her arms. She stares at him. Lightning flickers as images from that fateful day, 4 April 1968, begin to seep through the hotel walls.

Camae
The Prince of Peace. Shot.
His blood stains the concrete outside Room 306
A worker wipes away the blood but not before
Jesse baptizes his hands on the balcony
The baton passes on

More and more images of the American experience consume the walls as the hotel begins to disintegrate right before their very eyes.

Memphis burning
DC burning
 Cities burning
Vietnam burning
Coffins coming home
Another Kennedy killed
The baton passes on

Bayard Rustin
Stonewall Riots
Andrew Young
Julian Bond
Bob Marley
Redemption Songs
Angela Davis
Assatta Shakur
Afro picks
Black raised fists
Olympics
The baton passes on

The images have picked up in speed and the hotel continues to float away. It's almost as if **King** *is surrounded by the images, walking through the future that he will never inhabit.*

Camae
White children
Black children
Crayola-color children
Together in a cafeteria

Roots
The Jeffersons Sidney Poitier Superfly
Isaac Hayes
James Brown
I'm black and I'm PROUD!

Jesse for President
I am Somebody!

Camae *begins to float away into another world. Another*
dimension. Her voice becoming an echo as the future continues to
consume the stage.

Camae
Crips
Bloods
Blue
Red
White
Crack
Smack
Marion Barry
Tracks
AIDS
Reagan wins again

Berlin Walls
Apartheid falls
Robben Island sets Mandela free
Rodney King screams:
'Can't we all just get along?'
The baton passes on

No peace in the Middle East
Ruby Dee
'You sho'll is ugly!'
Spike Lee
Rwanda bleeds
Bill Clinton
Niggah please

Skinheads
The Cosby Show
Baby Mamas
Soul Train

Montelle
Don't Ask Don't Tell

Run DMC
BET
MTV
Walk this way
The baton passes on

And on and on
Till the break of dawn
For the American song
We shall overcome

A white Bronco flees into the night
If it doesn't fit, you must acquit

James Byrd
Columbine
Ron Brown
Colin Powell
Clarence Thomas
Tupac
Oprah
Biggie
Crack Corners
From Crenshaw
To MLK Boulevard

Saddam Hussein
Osama
George Bush
Condi Rice

The Towers sigh
The world turns gray
September 11th
One bright morning day

Katrina, Katrina
American as apple pie

Drove the Chevy to the levee
But the levee was drowned
The Superdome

Drive-bys
McDonald's
Diabetes Iraq
NBA
High-paid slaves
The children of the Nile
A nuclear 8 Mile
Black picket fences
And Jena Six
American flags
And Black Presidents!!!

The baton passes on
The baton passes on
The baton passes on
The baton passes on

The good, the bad and the ugly of America continue to proceed
like a fluid mental freeway into the very edge of now and perhaps
beyond. It's like a river with no levee and the images flood our
senses, our *minds, and* our *hearts. The sound and the fury of it*
all rises to a frenetic peak until BOOM! CRICKLE! CRICKLE-
CRACK!! A flash of lightning illuminates the stage. And suddenly
King *stands in the deep dark blue of the blackness, trying to take*
his rightful place in the universe among the stars. He is looking
over our *heads. Past us, through us, floating above us in the*
silence.

King (*in utter amazement*)   What is this vision I see before me?
Could this be my wildest dream? (*Taking it all in.*) There it is.
There . . . It . . . Is

A land where hunger is no more. A land where war is no more. A
land where richness is no more, poverty is no more, color is . . .
no more. Destruction . . . is no more. Only love. Fierce radical
love. The Promised Land here on Earth.

I accept. I will never walk through that blessed garden over yonder . . . that lush land just on the far side of moon. It . . . is . . . so . . .

King's *mouth cannot articulate his dream. For one he is speechless . . . He looks at his congregation from the mountaintop. With tears in his eyes, he gathers the strength to speak on.*

Well . . . nobody said it was gonna be easy. Nobody said it would happen in an instant. Everybody said we'd never get there. But then again nobody thought we'd make it this far. Can I get an Amen? I said can I get an Amen!

You have wandered the desert. The flaming sands burning your feet. But you are standing at the edge of Canaan on a mountaintop made of the dreams of men and women who have paid the ultimate price with their lives. Children of Nile you must rise, as you can no longer walk weary through this world with willowed backs. Your time is now, I tell you NOW!!

The baton may have been dropped. But anyone can pick it back up. I don't know where in the race we are, but pick up that baton and pass, pass, pass it along! This baton is no longer the burden my image can bear.

For, you are the climbers, the new carriers of the cross. I beg you, implore you, don't give in and toss it off. On this here mountaintop there is beauty to behold, the Promised Land your Promised Land in black, red, white, blue, brown and gold. Canaan is calling! She is calling for you to come!! The Promised Land is so close, and yet so far away, so close and yet so far away so close and yet so –

In a small pinpoint of light **Camae**'s *hand comes from behind* **King***, settling on his trembling shoulder.*

Camae   Time.

Blackout.

Notes

24   *sanitation workers* – trash collectors who went on strike in 1968 seeking safer working conditions and higher pay.

26   *Mason Temple* – large church named after Bishop Charles Harrison Mason, in Memphis, Tennessee, where Martin Luther King, Jr., delivered his 'Promised Land' or 'Mountaintop' speech on the eve of his assassination.

27   *Churches ain't even safe for us folks* – a reference to the 1963 bombing of 16th Street Baptist Church in Birmingham, Alabama, which killed four little girls and injured more than a dozen people.

31   *Yolanda . . . the boys . . . Goodnight, Bernice* – the names of King's daughters. His children were Dexter, Yolanda, Bernice and Martin III.

31   *Coretta Scott K* – Coretta Scott King, wife of Martin Luther King, Jr.

35   *April 4th?* – the date in 1968 when Martin Luther King, Jr., would be assassinated.

38   *Larry Payne* – teenager who was shot to death by a police officer in Memphis in 1968 after a peaceful demonstration turned violent.

40   *Alla God's children got wings* – traditional African American spiritual. Lyrics include 'All God's children got wings / When I get to heaven I'm goin' to put on my wings'.

41   *Andy or, better yet, Jesse* – Andy Young and Jesse Jackson were aides to Martin Luther King, Jr.

42   *drowned by hoses . . . bitten by dogs* – as people marched peacefully down streets across America in a campaign for civil rights, they were occasionally attacked by white residents and police officers who sprayed them

with fire hoses or confronted by barking (and sometimes) biting dogs.

43   *blowin' up children* –   a reference to the
      1963 Birmingham church bombing.

45   *don't need no PhD to give you some knowledge* –
      Martin Luther King, Jr., received his PhD in theology in
      1955 from Boston University.

46   *Malcolm X* –   prominent civil rights leader who
      advocated for a 'by any means necessary' tactic to
      dismantling segregationist and white supremacist culture.
      He was assassinated in 1965 at the age of thirty-nine.

47   *Speak by the sword, die by the sword* –   quoting the
      Bible (Mt. 26. 52); line is followed by Jesus advocating
      for the need for non-violent, peaceful solutions.

49   *Michael! Michael! MICHAEL!* –   birth name of Martin
      Luther King, Jr.

51   *Sending tapes to my wife* –   The American Federal
      Bureau of Investigation (FBI) spied on King and secretly
      recorded him. On one occasion, they sent evidence of an
      extramarital affair involving King to his wife, Coretta
      Scott King.

59   *Poor People's Campaign* –   the social movement King
      led to address economic inequality and poverty within
      the United States.

60   *Jericho Road* –   a long winding road that connected
      Jerusalem and Jericho where robbers often awaited
      travelers; a metaphor for looming danger.

61   *stabbed in my chest* –   Martin Luther King, Jr., was
      stabbed by a woman in 1958 with a letter opener in
      Harlem (New York City).

63   *St Augustine* –   highly influential Christian theologian
      who lived in the late fourth century.

65   *I've flown too close to the sun* –   reference to the myth of
      Icarus, who fashioned wings connected by wax, became
      overly confident in his abilities and flew higher and
      higher until the sun rays melted the wax, causing Icarus
      to plunge to his death.

66   *Ya Dig?* –   colloquialism for 'do you understand?'

66   *Black Panther* –   The Black Panther Party for Self
      Defense, founded in 1966, was established as a
      next-generation alternative to the civil rights efforts
      represented by King. The attire and rhetoric were, at
      times, more militaristic. Black Panthers celebrated
      Blackness and advocated for the importance (and
      necessity) of distinctly Black spaces and organizations.

67   *Ezekiel* –   a Hebrew prophet whose dreams contained
      prophecies.

73   *Jesse baptizes his hands* –   Jesse Jackson, Martin
      Luther King Jr.'s aide, dipped his hands in the blood of
      King and, later, appeared with blood-stained clothing.

73–77 *The Prince of Peace. Shot . . . Black Presidents.*
      – references to the legacy of King and the presidency
      (2009–17) of Barack Obama, the United States' first (and
      to date only) African American president.

78   *Children of the Nile* –   people of African descent. This
      phrase refers to a verse from *The Bible* (Exod. 1.22):
      'Every son born to the Hebrews you must throw into the
      Nile, but every daughter you may allow to live.'